TH

CHURCH

A SOCIAL MEDIA COMMUNICATION STRATEGY GUIDE
FOR CHURCHES, NONPROFITS AND INDIVIDUALS IN MINISTRY

NATCHI LAZARUS

www.theconnectedchurch.org

First Edition 2017
ISBN-13: 978-1543013818

Publication Data
Lazarus, Natchi
The Connected Church: A Social Media Communication Strategy Guide for Churches, Nonprofits and Individuals in Ministry
Natchi Lazarus – 1st ed.
ISBN-10: 1543013813

Dedicated to

Every believer who courageously took an unknown path
with childlike faith and unshakeable conviction in order
to serve others and build God's kingdom of love, simply
because they heard and obeyed the Father's call.

CONTENTS

FOREWORD
by Mark W. Schaefer

Social media keynote speaker, college educator, consultant, and best-selling author of six marketing books including Known, The Content Code, Social Media Explained and The Tao of Twitter
www.BusinessesGROW.com

I had been warned.

"You are entering a very dysfunctional world," my friend said. "Media outreach and communication strategies in the Christian world are probably out of step with what you're accustomed to in the business world."

And he was right.

My friend had invited me to address a conference of global missionaries dedicated to working on digital Christian outreach.

As an experienced communication and marketing professional from the secular world, I was excited to help however I could and learn about the opportunities and successes in the mission field. I had spent the last decade consulting on digital strategy with some of the biggest companies on the planet, and I was enthused about putting these skills to work in the name of our Lord.

But over the months and then years, I became disheartened by the tangle of out-of-date strategies and insufficient practices being deployed. Everyone's heart was in the right place, but it was too challenging for my brothers and sisters to keep up with the relentless pace of the digital world on top of their other pressing responsibilities.

My assessment was that the missionary professionals were at least five years behind the best practices of the business world, and in some cases, even more. As I became more involved in this work on both a global level and local church level, I saw this pattern repeated over and over again: people with limited resources hopelessly trying to keep up with a media landscape evolving at a breakneck pace.

I'll never forget the comment of one Christian leader who came up to me after following some of my advice for a year: "Mark, I'm happy to report we have moved our digital communications from pathetic to mediocre!"

We were not moving fast enough or reaching enough people, and I was beginning to feel overwhelmed myself. How could I even begin to make a dent in this problem? I felt deeply that Jesus would not want His Church to be "dysfunctional." We needed help.

That help has finally arrived, and it is in your hands.

The seed for this book was planted on a sunny park bench in Bangalore, India. My friend Natchi Lazarus and I had spent a lovely day walking through the gardens of the city's most famous botanical park. As we rested on the bench, he began to tell me about the wildly successful digital outreach he had engineered for his church. I was awed and inspired! I was so impressed, in fact, that I asked him if I could take out my smartphone and create a video of his success story. I still use that video as a case study in my college classes and corporate workshops today.

Natchi and I agreed that there was a colossal knowledge gap that needed to be filled in the global Church. How could we reproduce Natchi's success and scale it to every parish and ministry? One of the options we discussed was a book aimed at digital communication best practices specifically for the Church. This seemed to be a natural solution because a book would be complete, accessible anywhere and affordable to all.

I'm delighted that Natchi had both the vision and resolve to see it through. The Holy Spirit has moved him in a powerful way!

Now it's up to you.

Today, most of the world gets their news and information through social media. We have no choice but to be there, too, in a helpful, compassionate and loving way.

A straightforward, actionable plan to spread the Good News to the modern world is in your hands... but it still requires commitment and constancy of effort. Digital excellence is achievable with your focus and resolve.

My prayers are with you. May God's boundless love guide you and strengthen you on your digital journey.

Mark W. Schaefer

INTRODUCTION
by Rev. Sam P. Chelladurai

Senior Pastor of AFT Church and one of the most
influential Bible teachers in India
www.revsam.org

The Internet and social media have brought us into an age of unprecedented freedom and possibilities. The command of Jesus to 'go into all the world and preach the good news' is possible now more than ever. Our job as they say is 'to go where the people are'. Today, the Internet and social media is the place where the people are by the millions.

The reach of this medium is already surpassing that of television and other media. In the past years, churches and Christian ministries have made full use of the radio and television media to present the good news. Even in that I think we got in late because of our suspicion of such media. We thought that only evil could come out of them, so that some of us even refused to use these devices in our homes and forbade others from using them! But later we began to realize the potential of such media and started using them. Nowadays, even those who previously preached against television are appearing on television, asking people to remember to watch their programs regularly! When it came to computers and the Internet, our suspicion was even greater. Some of us even declared that it signaled the dawn of the Antichrist. But today we are once again realising the tremendous potential of this media and beginning to use it.

The situation now is that if we do not use Internet and social media, we will be a 'disconnected' Church - cut off from the very people we need to reach, because the masses out there are 'connected' to this media.

Natchi's book *The Connected Church* informs us about the potential and the possibilities that this media presents. Natchi has up-to-date knowledge of this field. More importantly, he has put this knowledge to practice with tremendous success when he got involved with our church and showed us how to use the Internet and social media effectively. Starting with the launch of a website for our church, he led us into the creation of a mobile app and the use of social media channels like YouTube, Facebook, Twitter, Instagram, Snapchat, Pinterest and Periscope.

Through his initiative, all our church services are now available LIVE on our website, YouTube channel, Facebook page and Periscope. So today as we preach in our church, we are at the same time addressing multiplied thousands of people who watch from all over the world. On our website, mobile app and social media channels, helpful video, audio and written resources are made available free worldwide to those who seek and search for guidance in their spiritual life. It is through this experience of designing and implementing a digital ministry program for us that Natchi became passionate about the use of this media for the work of the ministry.

Today, crossing all physical, national and cultural boundaries, we are able to reach people and provide 'real solutions' to their problems, because all human problems have a spiritual origin. People, who apart from social media would have no access to these spiritual resources, often share with us how their lives have been blessed and transformed because we were able to reach them through this media.

I believe this book will teach, educate and inspire churches and individuals in ministry to stay connected with the modern day masses that crowd around the Internet and social media, and help many who are out there searching desperately for the answers to their problems.

God has certainly given us an amazing open door through technology these days. I hope this book will help the reader see it and use it effectively.

In Him,
Sam P. Chelladurai

PREFACE

King George Square in Brisbane, Australia, was buzzing with activity. I stepped out of my hotel in Ann Street and felt the cold breeze of July and the mild sunshine on my face at the same time. It was a perfect Sunday evening to explore this vibrant city. I started walking towards the square, blissfully unaware of the fact that I was about to encounter three individuals who would inspire me to write this book – visual triggers that would encourage me to push harder towards my calling as a digital marketer and motivate me for a long time to come.

TRIGGER 1: THE SINCERE PREACHER

As I walked towards the square I came to a junction where a man was standing in a corner of the street with a Bible in his hands, preaching about the love of Jesus Christ. He appeared to be in his late 50s, dressed smartly in a business suit. He was obviously passionate about the Bible and comfortably at ease as he spoke. It clearly wasn't his first time preaching on the street.

Earlier that morning, I had shared God's word in the Sunday service at the Anglican church in Brisbane. As a public speaker and marketplace minister, I was curious to hear what the preacher on the street had to say. I have had the privilege of speaking in churches, conferences, seminars, summits and small groups but I've never had a chance to do street preaching. So I was fascinated by it and stood there listening.

He was good. He was expressive but not too extreme. He had good understanding of the scriptures, made sense and was presenting his thoughts coherently. He was telling people why it was a smart thing to follow Christ and how God can help anyone overcome any challenge when they decide to enter into a relationship with Him, through Jesus Christ. The preacher's body language was inviting, and he conveyed his message in an interesting and engaging style. He was doing a good job.

But there was one problem.

I was the only one listening to him.

Even though the square was crowded and buzzing with activity, I was the only person listening to him.

TRIGGER 2: THE TALENTED MUSICIAN

After listening to the street preacher, I walked a bit farther. I came across a young musician who was playing her flute beautifully. Peaceful, mild, magical notes flowed effortlessly out of her instrument, blending wonderfully with the weekend mood and cool evening breeze. She was enjoying herself and obviously wanted others to enjoy her gift and talent as well.

But there was one problem.

I was the only one listening to her.

TRIGGER 3: THE PASSIONATE SALESMAN

Just a few yards down the path from the musician, I came to a salesman promoting a special offer outside his shop. He loudly announced the price drop while organising his products on a makeshift shelf. He was funny. He talked about the quality of his products and boasted about his years of experience in this field. His price had dropped by 50% compared to the previous day, so it seemed like a good deal. It deserved the attention of at least a few people.

But there was one problem.

Yes, you guessed it right, I was the only one listening to him.

THE PUZZLE

The communicator in me was struck by these three encounters. What was wrong? Why were these three talented communicators unable to get the attention of their audience? The square was filled with people, but no one stopped to listen to them. All three of them seemed to possess something of value and were obviously talented in their fields. They were communicating in an engaging and interesting style, and they all seemed to be convinced that they were doing the right thing by sharing something good with their fellow countrymen. Yet, no one was listening to them. Neither the life-saving message of salvation nor the beautiful music nor the money-saving discount was able to grab the attention of the audience in that square that evening. Why?

As a marketing professional, I'm always curious about audience behaviour. I believe that a good product or message always attracts the right audience – one that knows good stuff from bad stuff. So I started thinking about why people were indifferent to these three communicators sharing particularly good stuff.

You might ask, 'Come on! Do you really expect people to stand and listen to a street preacher on a Sunday evening? Or a busker? Or a sales guy?'

I totally understand that reaction. But here are some considerations that made me think more deeply about this situation:

- It was a slow Sunday evening, not a Monday morning when people would be rushing to work. Most of the people in the square were just strolling.
- The weather was good, and people seemed relaxed.
- The street was only for pedestrians and cyclists, with no motor vehicle traffic allowed.

- Two of the communicators were not selling anything or asking people to take their wallets out. They were just sharing something good with people.

- Perhaps the preacher's sermon or the salesman's loud voice was not attractive to people, but what about the young musician? Why wasn't she able to attract an audience with her music?

I would have understood if just a few passers-by slowed down, stood there for a couple of seconds, listened to the three communicators and then moved on, having decided that it was not something that they liked to hear. That is a personal choice. But my concern arose from the fact that not a single person stopped to listen. No one stopped for even a second to consider what was being said or played. People just kept walking past the three as though they did not exist. That is what puzzled me.

SOLVING THE PUZZLE: THE REVELATION

After a few minutes of standing in the square, thinking about what I'd observed, looking for clues to solve the puzzle and keenly watching the crowd, I finally figured out the reason why people were not pausing to listen to the three communicators. It was there all the time, right in front of my eyes, and I did not see it.

Most passers-by could not have listened to the communicators even if they had wanted to. In fact, they couldn't listen to anyone or anything.

Why? Because most of them were already listening to something else, with *headphones* on or *earbuds* plugged into their ears.

Duh!

This may not seem like a profound discovery, but it was a very significant moment from a marketing communications perspective and a revelation of sorts for me as a communicator of my faith. I realised this: Whether you are a teacher, a preacher, an entertainer or a salesman, the dynamics of how you communicate with your audience have completely changed.

We are in a new era of communication.

It's not about a speaker or a message anymore, but rather it's about the medium that they use for communication. Even if the greatest orator or award-winning singer or highest-grossing salesperson had been standing in the square that evening, they could not have made the people listen to them because something else was already occupying their ear-space and, in turn, their mind-space.

That audience's attention was already claimed by the devices that were powering their headphones. Maybe they were listening to music or podcasts or a live message on social media. If the communicators had somehow managed to get their messages or music into those devices in the palm of each person's hands, then they would have had a chance of being heard. For example, if the street preacher could package his message as a podcast or a live video and distribute it to smartphones, iPads and other devices, then he could be heard.

The communicators needed a new communication method and strategy.

THE NEW MEDIA REVOLUTION

I've realised that what I was witnessing in the square that evening was just an example of what's going on around the world. There is a new media revolution happening, and the Church isn't fully aware of it. We all know something is happening, but as a Church many of us are unable to locate the exact change and take full advantage of it.

We are in the age of the *headphone generation* that uses gadgets and devices to constantly update, comment, post, snap, tweet, chat and interact with the world electronically, letting images and videos occupy their mind-space and influence them. Communicating anything to this generation is a challenge if you're not part of the new media communication ecosystem. You need to understand how they communicate and adapt yourself.

In scriptures and throughout history we see how the Church has adapted itself and learned to use the relevant media of the age to communicate the love of God. The Church communicated its message initially through word-of-mouth, then they recorded it on goat skins, which then evolved to printed paper, then to computers, handheld devices and more recently software and the Internet.

Now we're in the middle of a new age: the Social Media Age. And it's time for us to evolve our communication strategy to remain relevant and effective.

The good news is that it *is* possible. And this book is all about that possibility.

THE PURPOSE OF THIS BOOK

The purpose of this book is to help you:

- Understand the current social media revolution.
- Lay a strong foundation for your social media ministry.
- Prepare for the technology changes of the future.

If you implement the strategies and framework that I outline, then by the end of this book you will have a strong social media foundation for your ministry. I am not saying that this book is all you need. But it is definitely a good starting point.

Each of us are called by God to use our unique gifts for a unique purpose. We each minister to our audience in unique ways. Some of us minister from our pulpits, while others minister from our office cubicles. Some of us help people know Christ by preaching in conferences, while others help people know Christ by quietly leading a life that displays the love of God in everyday situations. Some of us manage large Christian nonprofits, while others volunteer for a small role and offer time to help others. No matter how you are ministering to others, this book is designed to help you use social media effectively for that ministry. The strategies that I lay out are universal communication strategies that will work for any organisation or individual involved in any form of ministry.

INTRODUCING THE S.P.I.R.I.T. FRAMEWORK™

This book is based on the S.P.I.R.I.T. Framework™ that I developed and have used in many of my social media consulting assignments with large and small Christian organisations and businesses. It is a proven, practical, simple and effective tool that you can use to refine and strengthen your online communication strategy.

This book is organised into four sections:

Section I: Why the Church should use Social Media: In the first section I discuss the importance of using the digital, online and social communication medium. I explore the *connected* audience to whom you will be ministering to using social media, and I show you how suitable the Christian message is for the online medium (contrary to popular belief). I also look at the biblical basis of social media marketing and its relevance to The Great Commission given to all believers by Jesus.

Section II: The Communication Model: In the second section, I introduce the *Connected Church*

Communication Model™ as a way to strengthen communication within the Body of Christ. I lay out a broader vision of a smooth, seamless functioning of the Church as one body using social media and technology.

Section III: The Framework for Implementing the Communication Model: In the third section, we move from visioning mode to action mode. We focus on the S.P.I.R.I.T. Framework™ as a practical way to implement the Connected Church Communication Model™ in your ministry. This is a hands-on implementation section that examines management strategies, marketing strategies and operational details.

Section IV: Future Trends that will Impact the Church: In the fourth and final section, we return to visioning mode as I identify trends for the future and ways you can prepare your ministry for the coming changes and challenges. You can think of this as a prophetic section of the book where we carefully and prayerfully try to peek into the future, examine trends and seek God's guidance on how to prepare your ministry for the coming days.

PROVEN, PRACTICAL STRATEGIES

The communication model, strategies, plans and thoughts that I present in this book are ones that I have personally used and successfully implemented as part of my work. They are not just theories. They are practical strategies that I have evolved and fine-tuned over time. And they can be implemented right away.

I am a member of Apostolic Fellowship Tabernacle[1], Chennai one of the fastest growing churches in India, and I have worked in the technology initiatives of my church, for more than 10 years now. I have seen major Kingdom impact that our church has created around the world because of its readiness to adapt to emerging media. We were one of the first churches in India to produce a live webcast. We started video and audio streaming all our Sunday services live on the internet using a 2G USB Dongle that was able to stream only at a very low bit rate. It didn't look as great as it does today, but it did reach thousands of people and bless them. Some of our other early initiatives with technology include releasing a mobile app and using it to livestream our services when smartphones were just starting to come into usage, communicating using social media as early as 2006 (just two years after Facebook was launched), publishing online magazines, accepting online donations, enabling people to send online prayer requests, creating a dedicated tech support team, audio streaming services, producing podcasts, creating online TV and radio channels and more.

Our senior pastor Rev. Sam P. Chelladurai is very tech-savvy; it never ceases to amaze me how he remains open to new technologies and is always ready to experiment. He has seldom rejected any of my suggestions to experiment with the next big social media techniques and tools. His heart is always ready to reach people and minister to them using relevant methods, the latest trends and the most effective medium of communication. I thank God for His grace and divine plan in leading me to this church at the right time; it's where I grew not only as a Christian learning the principles of God's word, but also as a digital marketer working on various technologies that has helped the church share the Good News to millions.

My work in our church's technology division has helped me witness firsthand the impact online communication tools and social media can create for the Kingdom of God. We grew our social media following by sharing value-added content and implementing techniques that I outline later in this book. At the time of writing this book, our church building may only hold a couple of thousand people at any given time, but we have at least 10 times as many viewers online each week watching our live services on our website and social media channels. Our online congregation has become much bigger than our offline congregation, and it is growing exponentially even as you read this.

I would like to make an important point here: the reason for our church's successful social media ministry is not just our online techniques – it is also the quality of the content. Content quality and marketing techniques go hand in hand. One will not be effective without the other. Without the valuable, powerful, well-researched, well-delivered and life-transforming content of our pastor's sermons (and the power of God behind it), all our technology and social media marketing efforts would not have produced the results we've seen. Only value-adding content can be effectively amplified. The audience always recognises a good message when they see one.

A good seed always produces good harvest. Social media marketing is a seed that takes time to cultivate but eventually produces sweet, abundant and satisfying fruit for all the labour that goes into it. We have received hundreds of incredible testimonies from people around the world who benefit every day from the online initiatives of our church. We have heard testimonies of people listening to our church messages in war zones and being encouraged. We have had people tell us that our livestream is the only church within hundreds of miles of where they live. They even invite their neighbours to come to church with them and worship every week right in their living room, projecting the live webcast of our church services on their TV screens. People who live great distances from our church remain connected to the organisation because of technology and social media. They write to us, talk to us, participate, pray and interact with us just like other church members. They consider it no different than being physically present in the church as members. And when we organise events or seminars in their areas, they gather in large numbers to meet and fellowship with us. These days when our pastor decides to minister in a particular town or city, we hardly do any promotions for the event. We just announce it on social media, thousands of people sign up for the event and the seats are booked in a matter of hours.

In this book I am happy to share with you the key strategies that have worked for my church's online ministry. I will show you how you can implement them successfully for your ministry. This framework will meet the online communication needs of any Christian organisation irrespective of the denomination.

How to Use This Book

If you're a ministry that hasn't started using social media yet, you can use this book as a workbook to start your digital marketing journey. If you've dipped your toe into the social media marketing pool and would like to increase your effort and activities, working on these strategies will help you, too.

I suggest that you follow these simple steps:

1. Get your core team involved.
2. Assign one person to lead the initiative.
3. Go through the S.P.I.R.I.T. Framework™ section by section.
4. Use the additional free support material and resources available on the connected church website (details below).

If you're already working on digital media and social media marketing, and you need guidance on a specific topic, simply look up that topic in the table of contents and review that section with your core team.

We all get stuck at some point in our online communication journey. And social media is always changing and evolving. When you're stuck, you can refer to this framework and fix the problem that got you stuck. For example, you may be getting a lot of traffic to your website, but people are not commenting, writing or engaging with you. You could turn to Chapter 10 where we discuss 'content ignition' strategies and implement some of them.

GIFT THIS BOOK

You may know of churches, preachers, missionaries or ministers who are very good at and committed to their calling, but they may not be good with using social media or they may not be good at promoting themselves and their ministry online. And maybe you've thought, '*I wish more people knew about this wonderful ministry,*' but didn't know how to get the word out. This book is a tool to help them. Gift this book to them and connect them to my website where there are teaching resources that walk ministries through the process, step by step, of reaching a wider audience. You can visit www.theconnectedchurch.org/tccbook/gift if you wish me to send copies of this book to specific organisations as your gift.

A NOTE ABOUT TERMINOLOGY

Throughout this book, for better communication and understanding, I use certain words with certain meanings

Ministry – I use this one word, *ministry*, to represent churches, missionaries, para church organisations, Christian nonprofits, marketplace ministers, elders, individuals in ministry and even Christian businesses that consider their business to be ministry. In other words, the word *ministry* in this book represents any person or organisation that is trying to proclaim the Good News of Jesus Christ with or without using words and symbols.

Church – Whenever I use the word *Church* with a capital letter C, I talk about the Body of Christ which encompasses every individual who believes in Jesus Christ as their Lord and Saviour. This is not the church as an organisation or a building.

church – When I use the term *church* (without capital letters, unless a sentence begins with the word), I am talking about the church as an organisation or a building.

ONLINE RESOURCES

In addition to this book, I have made available an extensive collection of videos, blog posts, step-by-step practical guides, tutorials, actionable tips and techniques, podcasts, webinars, expert interviews, email resources, online courses, ebooks, events details and more online.

Visit www.theconnectedchurch.org to access all of the resources.

Now let us start this exciting journey.

www.theconnectedchurch.org

SECTION 1

WHY THE CHURCH SHOULD USE SOCIAL MEDIA

CHAPTER 1

THE CONNECTED AUDIENCE

What if Jesus Christ was on social media? Imagine that social media existed when he was on earth, as a man, ministering to people. Do you think the greatest communicator ever to have lived would have used a tool like social media for his ministry and to connect with his audience?

- What would Jesus' profile pictures look like?
- Would he be tweeting about his ideas, thoughts and opinions?
- Would 'Sermon on the mount' be a blog post on his website?
- How would he use LinkedIn to connect with professionals?
- Would Jesus be on Snapchat?
- Would the resurrection of Lazarus be streamed live on Periscope by someone who witnessed it?
- Imagine a YouTube video of Jesus walking on water. How viral would that go?

As followers of Christ, one thing we should do is to try to model ourselves and our behaviour after Jesus. So imagining such scenarios is not blasphemous. In fact, one of the best ways to grow as a Christian is to imagine what Christ would do in circumstances that you face in everyday life. So when we consider using social media for our ministry, it is helpful to imagine what Jesus would have done with social media for his ministry. And it's important to examine his approach to ministry during his lifetime on earth for principles that we can learn from.

I do think that if social media channels were available in Jesus' time, he would have used them to the fullest capacity for his ministry.

How do I know that? The Bible provides a clue.

A little bit of research will show you that Jesus was a unique preacher for his time. When all the rabbis and teachers were teaching in synagogues and religious locations where people gathered on particular days, Jesus had the habit of preaching and teaching in the common marketplace where people gathered to work and do business every day. Of the 132 public appearances of Jesus in the Bible, 122 were in the marketplace[1]. Of the 52 parables of Jesus, 45 of them involved work and the marketplace. Remember the parable of the sower? Agriculture was the IT industry of Jesus' time. It was the main driver of the economy in those days. Fishing, cattle rearing and agriculture would have been the top three industries of his time. And Jesus chose to illustrate his teaching with examples from these industries. He wanted people to relate to his message practically. He wanted them to understand what he was saying in the context of their everyday life. He was a very practical, appealing and relevant teacher.

And most of the time he delivered these teachings right in the middle of the marketplace because that is where people were. That was Jesus' style of communication. He was not interested in hanging around in high, lofty and holy places; he loved to be in the midst of his people, in the midst of their everyday life situations and challenges.

This is a key lesson for us.

As ministers we should go to where the people are, reach out to them and minister to them in the midst of their everyday lives. We should not build our own little system and then try to make people come into it. Many times church ministers and church leaders ask me, 'Natchi, how do I use social media and technology to get more people to come into my church?' or 'How do I use online marketing to get people to come to my conferences or seminars?' My question back to them is, 'Just like Jesus, why don't you think about going to places where people are already spending their time, and minister to them and serve them there?' Think about that. Selah!

Today one of the best ways to establish your presence where the people are is by being present on social media. At the time of this writing, out of the total 7.3 billion people in this world, 3.17 billion are on the internet and

2.3 billion are actively using social media networks[2]. Do you think Jesus would want us to miss this opportunity to communicate to and serve 2.3 billion people by ignoring social media? I don't think so.

I think he would want us to get on social media every day and bless people with value-adding messages and Bible-based teachings, edifying them and encouraging them with the principles of the Word of God. Just like in Jesus' time, when thousands of people gathered in marketplaces, today billions of people virtually gather in electronic marketplaces using their mobile devices and social media apps. We as ministers need to be in the midst of them. If we do that, then we are modelling our ministry after Jesus. And when you do that over a period of time, you will see your church buildings and conferences fill up for each event and gathering. It's time to start thinking differently about reaching people.

THE EVOLUTION OF AUDIENCES

The way audiences process information has changed more in the last 10 years than it had in the last 1,000+ years. Our technological progress has given birth to a new generation of audience. I like to call them the *connected audience*. Powered by global connectivity and affordable smartphones, they have a unique way of receiving and processing information. Developing the right social media strategy requires a deep understanding of this new audience and their behaviour.

Before we focus on the connected audience, you need to understand the five types of audience that are key to any ministry. You need to consider these audiences and their behaviour while planning your communication strategy.

The Face-to-Face Live Audience

For many years, right from Jesus' time, most ministry happened face-to-face. Jesus ministered in front of a live audience. In the early Church, sermons, prayer sessions, evangelical meetings, counselling sessions and all other types of ministry happened in front of a live audience. And before leaving, Jesus prepared his disciples to go out into the world and plant more churches in person, so that more people could be ministered to. Thomas had to travel all the way to India from the Middle East – a journey that might have taken months. That is how the Gospel spread across the world – face-to-face, one-on-one – and this type of ministry continues to be relevant and important for church growth.

Even though I am a digital marketing consultant, I am also a big believer in the power of personal interactions. When human beings get together and meet in person, there are spiritual dynamics at work that can never be replaced by any other type of interaction. While online media, gadgets and social networking channels have their roles to play (as I discuss in the rest of the book) I believe that God still wants us to be more human and connect with each other in person as much as possible. That is why in-person ministry remains very effective, even with all the social media and technology available. Nothing can replace an in-person interaction.

But in-person ministry can be limited by time and space. And there are elements of ministry like teaching, prayer and counselling that can be done effectively in a remote setting as well. So we need to find the correct mix of technology-driven components, remote ministry components and in-person ministry components.

The On-demand Audience

The art of recording God's principles for reference started very early – we see God himself writing the 10 commandments on a tablet for Moses in Mount Sinai. But after the printing technology evolved, the written word started spreading at a much faster rate. With the advancement of flat-bed printing in the 15th century and electronic media including the telegraph and telephone in the 18th century, the Church started to see a new breed of audience, and I like to call them the *on-demand audience*.

This audience chose to access the word of God and ministry resources whenever they wanted to using on-demand media. The on-demand audience is a big part of the Church communication system today; this audience still buys magazines, books, tapes, CDs and DVDs and accesses them whenever they want to. The latest technologies that cater to this type of audience are the mp3 and mp4 files distributed on flash drives, memory cards, direct downloads of files and cloud storage.

The Broadcast Audience

The evolution of radio and TV technology gave birth to the *broadcast audience*. They listen to radio programs and watch TV programs when they are broadcast at a particular time. They make note of the time of broadcast and tune in. This audience exists in large numbers even today, and they are still relevant and important. But we are seeing a change in the behaviour of this type of audience as TV and radio technology starts to merge with the internet. Today, smart TVs are internet-enabled, TV shows and radio programs are streamed live online or on TV using the internet and devices like the Apple TV and Roku player are further bridging and shrinking the gap between a computer and television. Without getting too technical, it is safe to say that TV and radio technologies are going through a major transformation and will continue to evolve. Eventually we will see television as a medium powered mostly by the internet. But despite all this, the broadcast audience is still worthy of your attention.

The Online Audience

Internet technology started evolving in 1950s, but only in the late 80s and early 90s did we see an accelerated growth in the internet-enabled online media. This gave birth to the *online audience* who uses the internet to consume information. This is the audience that visits your website and consumes information that you make available there, reading your online publications, sending emails to your ministry and researching your work. They are comfortable using software and hardware on a daily basis. Thanks to smartphones and tablets, this audience is now accessing the internet on their mobile devices. This audience plays a big role in many of our discussions throughout this book. Many of the foundational steps that I discuss, like website building, mobile app development and using IT in your regular ministry operations, will help you minister to this type of audience.

The Connected Audience

The new breed of audience that has emerged out of the combination of social media and mobile technology is the hero of our story and the central subject for the rest of this book. I call them the *connected audience*.

The reason I call them the connected audience is because they remain connected at all times. Internet connectivity is part of who they are. From the moment they wake up in the morning to the time they go to bed at night, their activities are centred around connectivity. They do not use their mobile devices just to check emails and make calls – they use their devices in almost all areas of their lives, from banking and shopping to communicating with friends and documenting important and not-so-important moments in their lives. This is the new breed of audience that you cannot afford to ignore.

I refer to the connected audience as a new breed and not a new generation. Even though younger generations are more tech-savvy and gadget-friendly than older generations, I do not agree with some experts who say that the need to be connected is limited to people of a certain age. The internet and social media have an impact on people of all generations. There is some value in classifying generations as X, Y and Z, but when it comes to social media, it is more accurate to classify the audience based on their behaviour and preference than their date of birth. For example, my mother-in-law who is over 70 years old prefers listening to our church service live on the internet than attending in person and regularly uses our church's mobile app to access YouTube videos of our sermons. Even though she is not as quick as my 10-year-old nephew on the iPad, behaviourally she still qualifies as part of the connected audience. Just like the other four types of audiences, the connected audience encompasses people of all age groups and socio-economic backgrounds.

AUDIENCE MIX IN THE COMMUNICATION ECOSYSTEM

In order to be effective in ministry, we need to understand the current communication ecosystem. The key components of this ecosystem are the sender, receiver, message, noise (surrounding distractions), medium and feedback mechanism. This is the classic communication model.

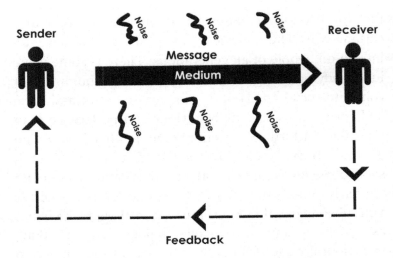

Even though this classic communication model remains fundamentally the same, each component is going through a sea change thanks to internet, social media and mobile technology. The receiver end is transformed into a mix of the five types of audiences that I discussed earlier in this chapter. The feedback mechanism is transformed completely to allow real time feedback between the sender and the receiver. The medium is now dominated by social media that is replacing TV, radio and print. The noise component is getting a lot of attention as content increases at a incredible rate. So almost all elements of this classic communication model are going through transformations due to the internet.

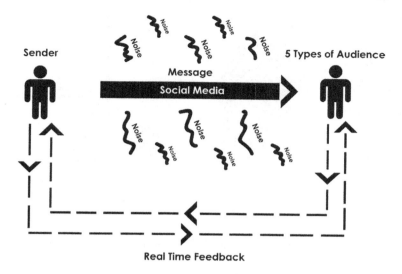

For now, let us focus on the audience mix.

In every period of history there has been a varied proportion of each type of audience in the mix. For example, long ago the face-to-face audience would have occupied a bigger portion compared to the other four types of audience. As technology evolved, the on-demand audience and the internet audience started to occupy more space within the communication ecosystem.

Today the connected audience is beginning to grow and occupy a very large piece of the pie. In the days to come this trend will only increase in the communication ecosystem of the Church. That is why it is important for us to understand this audience and adapt our communications strategy to them.

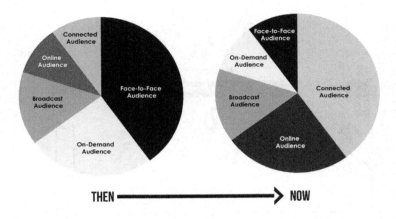

THEN ──────────────────────────▶ NOW

THE CHARACTERISTICS OF THE CONNECTED AUDIENCE

- **They have access to information.** The connected audience has access to all knowledge at the tips of their fingers. In other words, they know how to Google. This ability gives them confidence to look for answers to life's most difficult questions using their smartphones. They don't collect books, CDs, DVDs or dictionaries like the other types of audiences. When in doubt, they Google. If you have information or a message for this audience, your primary responsibility is to make that information 'searchable' so that you are found when they look for you.

- **They are eager to learn and research.** The connected audience is eager to learn. They are inquisitive and curious about things. They will spend hours diving deep into the subjects and topics that interest them. Research is part of their lifestyle. When they hear you speak about a topic in church, they might later Google it and find more answers if the topic is of interest to them. They will spend hours watching videos, reading blogs and going through online courses. You need to make available a lot of research material, resources and videos to help them learn more about the things you are trying to communicate about.

- **They are always connected.** The connected audience, as their name says, is always 'connected'. They are connected to each other, they are connected to your church, they are connected to your ministry and they are connected to the rest of the world. They become restless when they do not have connectivity. Research says[3] that an average person looks at their mobile phone 110 times a day! Connectivity is the heartbeat of this new breed of audience, and that poses both an opportunity and a challenge. Every time they look at their mobile devices, you have an opportunity to be visible to them, connect with them and communicate to them. But if you do not have the right presence or content, there are 1,000 things that can get their attention and take them far away from your message.

- **They are open to other opinions and points of view.** The connected audience is willing to discuss their faith and belief with others openly. They are not shy. They are confident in who they are and what they believe in. They are active on forums and in social media groups. Once they are convinced, they are open and willing to have a discussion even about things they do not understand well. They would rather talk about things and gain clarity than keep quiet. They are expressive by nature. They want to make sure they have had their say in all matters, but they are not judgmental about others' opinions. They accept them or ignore them, but they do not judge them (most of the time). They read more than one view on any subject.

- **They value convenience.** The connected audience wants and values convenience. They look for easier ways to get things done. And if you help them transact conveniently, they will continue to transact with you and stay connected to you. Make their life easier and you will be their best friend.

- **They are willing to be your brand ambassadors/evangelists.** The connected audience has no problem sharing information about you with their network and being an ambassador for your ministry. Jesus called us to be Ambassadors of the Kingdom; ministries need ambassadors – people who believe in the vision of a ministry and can be its brand ambassadors. If you work hard to stay connected to the connected audience and provide value to them constantly, they will have no problem being your ambassadors. They will talk about you in forums, blogs and social media. They will defend your point of view fearlessly, support you openly and stand by you faithfully.

- **They are not exclusively yours.** Even though they are a wonderful audience to have, you cannot have them all to yourself. With the connected audience, your view of ministry or church membership needs to change. The connected audience likes their freedom. They are free-spirited and interested in exploring multiple ministries, not because they are disloyal to you but because of their thirst for knowledge. They might be loyal and dedicated to your ministry, but that will not stop them from connecting to another ministry for some other purposes. Open your mind to that reality and develop a magnanimous, sharing attitude.

For example, I know many people who are members of one church but interact online with another church on a regular basis. Every Sunday, after coming home from their main church services, they watch the livestream from the second church on their mobile devices. They are loyal to their own churches, where they are members, but that does not stop them from accessing another church's material online. Perhaps the pastor of the second church was speaking on a topic that is rarely discussed in their main church, or he discussed it with a new perspective that they have not heard before. So, they find it beneficial. They even participate in events online, donate and buy products. In a way, they are members of multiple churches, and they want the best of whatever is available.

Many church leaders and ministers are frustrated when members of their congregations go to a different church even for one week. With technology and the internet, there is no way to stop someone from being part of any church and any denomination. In a way, I think it is something good and a much needed transformation in the Body of Christ. It truly make us ONE BODY in Christ. We cannot operate on our own little islands anymore. Gone are the days when people grew up as a member of one church or denomination and continued to be that all their life. There is nothing wrong with that, but it is a bigger joy to celebrate the differences that exists in different ministries and churches.

In fact, that is how the first Church was built: One person sowed the seed, the other watered it and another had the harvest. The early Church leaders did not consider any congregation their own. Social media and technology are returning us to that open model where people have the freedom to enjoy the gifts of various members of the Body of Christ. I am excited about the possibility that today the audience can be truly free and empowered by learning from various unique ministries. The audience always benefits when it consumes content from a ministry with a special revelation about a particular subject.

- **They appreciate uniqueness and value**. The connected audience appreciates the uniqueness of each ministry and individual, so communicate your uniqueness and your calling to your audience. This will help them understand you better and stay connected with you in order to get the most value.

Throughout this book we will continue to explore the characteristics of the connected audience and the various steps you can take to ensure that you are relevant and ready to minister to them. We are living in a time when we have an unprecedented opportunity to influence this generation in the right way, making them walk in the light. The ancient eternal principles of God's word can change the lives of millions of people if they are presented in the right manner. Leveraging that opportunity is in your hands and mine. If we don't take advantage of the opportunity, we may lose this audience forever. But if we wake up now and take the right steps to use social media to communicate the everlasting principles of God's word, then we can reach this generation.

CHAPTER 2

A SUITABLE MESSAGE

Are the Bible and the Christian message suitable for social media?

Is it possible to take the ancient Biblical truths and customise them for the modern digital age?

Social media is meant for people to share photos and business advertisements, right? Is it really a relevant medium for the Gospel?

These are some of the questions that I have been asked in conferences and seminars. My answer to them is *'Yes. Yes. And yes!'*

Whenever a new technology hits the market, the Church's first reaction is to think that it is relevant only for commercial purposes. It happened with radio, then TV and now it's happening with social media. When you look at all the posts, comments and conversations that exist in social media today, you may think it's not the right place to share details about your ministry, Bible concepts and principles. But that is far from the truth.

There are many reasons the Christian message and Bible truth are well-suited for social media. Here are the top 4, in my opinion.

THE BIBLE HAS ANSWERS.

Social media is not just about cat videos and vacation photos (even though they are all over the place). It's also a platform where the *connected audience* looks for answers to some of the most important questions in their life, work and relationships. Social media isn't just a place to browse photos of friends and family. It's also a place where people find information that influences their thoughts and actions.

Humans are social beings in need of affirmation and influence. We turn to our trusted sources, circle of friends and family for their opinions, and we like getting influenced by them. Think about the last time you bought a new mobile phone. You probably asked friends and family for their opinions, and you may have checked out online reviews. Over time we develop a set of trusted sources that give us the right answers to our questions. When we find that trusted source, we develop a habit of going to that source for answers.

In a way, you could call this the modern version of what the Bible calls the act of seeking 'Good Counsel' and 'Good Advice' (Proverbs 20:18). And I believe this is the way God wants us to live, as a community developing trust and relationships. Consider how Jethro came into Moses' life at the right time and gave him one piece of good advice. Without that crucial input from a trusted family member, Moses would have killed himself working hard day and night. So, as human beings, it is a good practice to take the help of trusted sources and our community to solve life's problems.

Social media is a great place for anyone to build a reputation of trust.

Now the question is this: As a ministry, would you like to be that trusted source that your community looks to for answers? Do you have answers that can help people? God has called you to ministry because you have the answer to someone's problem. Now you have to let that person know that you have the answers by spreading your answers on social media. This will help people who are looking for that solution to find it and benefit from it.

Consider today's teenagers. When they grow up in the absence of an open family or good friends, where do they go for answers to questions concerning relationships, sex, careers, leadership and finding life's purpose? They pick up their mobile devices and Google them, getting search results from social media and blog articles, and then those teens go to social media to see who has opinions and answers, and they're influenced by the responses. Some teenagers do not even openly type out these questions on the internet; instead they silently browse and look for conversations about these topics and get influenced by them. If you are a Christian ministry focusing on helping young people find life's purpose, this is a great opportunity for you to provide answers to teenagers seeking answers.

Godly answers help people turn to light instead of darkness. When people get answers to their pressing questions in a time of need, they're ready to accept truths that they previously ignored. Answers to questions provide a great context to the truth that is being presented. Irrespective of their background or the faith-environment in which they were brought up, if people see the answers to their key questions coming from the Bible, then they will have no problem accepting them.

But how do you share answers if you're not present on social media where the questions are being asked? That is why it is important to be present on social media. Your ministry must be there to present and provide the unique answers that God has given you to solve the unique problems of your audience.

Billions of questions are being asked on Google and Facebook every day[1]! In Chapter 1, I explain that the connected audience is so curious that they will not stop looking until they find answers to their questions. If we who are called for ministry fail to use our God-given answers to influence the billions of people on social media today, then we run the risk of losing these people to sources of influence that may not guide them in the right path.

THE BIBLE GIVES HOPE.

Many of the top posts on social media are quotes and stories of hope. People face many problems and challenging situations in their daily lives, and they are looking for hope, encouragement, motivation and practical advice to help them overcome these challenges and achieve what they want to achieve. They are looking for truths that will set them free and allow them to move forward.

What better source of encouragement than the Bible, and what better medium to present it than social media!

As ministers, we are all called not only to share the truth, but also to encourage each other. We carry the Good News that is entrusted in our hands: the eternal hope for mankind and this creation.

There are many ways in which you can give hope to your audience on social media. Share your own testimony. Share the stories and testimonies of people in your network or organisation. Testimonies are powerful. They encourage the audience by giving them hope. The Bible says[2], 'By the blood of the Lamb and the word of their Testimony they overcame the evil one.' Today, social media is the best place for you to share your testimony. By posting an encouraging story in one channel you can potentially help millions of people gain hope and motivation.

Browse your social media network and you will see that many viral videos consist of stories of people overcoming hardships, stories of people not giving up, stories of winners in the middle of impossible situations, stories of little Davids defeating the big Goliath-like problems in life. People love that kind of stuff, and we have the Bible full of such encouragement and hope. I cannot think of any better content than the Bible to impact the lives of people and give hope to humanity. More than a religious message, it is a message for humanity, offering hope of a sin-free, eternal, peaceful life. This message of hope can give strength to the weak, hope to the hopeless and light to those in the midst of darkness. When presented in a non-condemning, truthful, transparent and relevant manner, the core message of the Bible can help many who are suffering. Unlike some our predecessors in ministry, we have an opportunity to present this message of hope in a beautiful, accessible format using modern visual tools like video, audio, images, animation and much more on a powerful platform like social media.

THE BIBLE HAS GLOBAL RELEVANCE.

In social media, context is as important as content. When you share a message on social media, it has the potential to reach people around the world. So it's important to share content that is relevant to a global audience.

The Bible and the Christian message are meant for a global audience, so any basic principle that you share will be relevant to your audience. For example, I have a personal testimony of God helping me get out of an impossible debt situation. Even though that happened in India and many of my circumstances are Indian market-related, I find that when I share my story and talk about the Biblical principles that helped me overcome, I'm able to help people all over the world. The Biblical principles of overcoming financial debt make sense to everyone. Some details of implementation may vary, but the core principle remains the same. It is much easier for us in ministry to come up with content that has global appeal and relevance than it is for many businesses or commercial establishments.

I encourage you to be careful about the way you present your content. Even though the principles have a global appeal, you cannot ignore the cultural differences that exist around the world. Certain words, expressions and sentence construction that are acceptable in one part of the world may not make sense or might even be rude in another culture. So even though you have source material that is globally appealing and relevant, you must pay careful attention to the way in which you present it.

THE BIBLE IS SEARCH-FRIENDLY.

In the beginning was the Word[3].

The Christian message is based on words. In the days before the term *Christian* became popular, we were known as the *word people* or *people of the word,* which still rings true. All that we do as Christians is centred around the word of God, and our Lord Jesus himself is 'word made flesh.'

Social media and the internet are also all about words. How do we search for anything on Google or Facebook? Using a set of words. What is our website and social media content filled with? A set of words. The foundation of any information found on the internet is the word. The blogs we write, the posts we share, the videos we make, the images we design – they are all based on words. In fact, the most talked about subject in digital marketing is *keyword,* a term that is commonly used in Search Engine Optimisation (SEO). Many technology companies are hiring linguistic research scholars and literature experts, and content writers are in high demand. The entire technology-enabled connected world revolves around words.

That is why the Bible and social media are a perfect match. When millions of people are already being influenced by gazillions of generic words, imagine how much more they can influenced by God's word that is full of life and light. As ministries who have the Bible, a word-based source material, at the centre of all our social media campaigns, we have a big opportunity in the social media space.

In my experience as a consultant, I see that most of the time spent by businesses and commercial organisations on social media marketing goes toward coming up with the right set of words for their content. For ministries, the hard part is already done – we already have the right words. We just need to package them carefully and deliver them to our audience.

The other good thing about Christian content is the stories. Christian living is about testimonies and stories. And social media audiences love stories. If you are a church or a ministry, you have an incredible supply of stories from the Bible. You also have stories of your personal life and the impact that you have created in the lives of others. If you are a Christian nonprofit, you have stories of the impact that you have created in the lives of people that your organisation reaches out to. These stories are a great source of content. You can write blogs, create videos and design images based on them.

CHAPTER 3

THE GREAT COMMISSION

When Jesus gave the Great Commission in Matthew 28[1], he gave it to the Church as a whole – to all of us, not just pastors and preachers. Every believer of Jesus Christ is called to be in ministry, fulfilling the Great Commission irrespective of their profession, occupation, location or qualification. This final set of instructions given by Jesus before he left this world is recorded in the last three verses in the Book of the Gospel according to Matthew, and it gives us a clear mission statement for our time on this earth.

Social media can be an important tool to help us fulfil this mission. Thanks to the internet and social media, this generation is better equipped to fulfil the Great Commission than any other generation that ever existed. The phrase 'reaching the nations' sounds less daunting today than it did 100 years ago.

We use Facebook Messenger, Whatsapp and Snapchat almost daily to reach and communicate instantly with family, friends and colleagues who live on the other side of the world. Today, wherever you are you can use your smartphone to create a live video stream on a social media channel and 'disciple' your audience in any corner of the globe, 'teaching them to observe all things' that Jesus commanded them. We have the privilege and facility that great Apostles like Paul and Peter would have loved to have in their hands. But with privilege comes responsibility. We need to make full use of technology and social media to fulfil the Great Commission.

Let us take a closer look at the key components of the Great Commission given to us by our Lord Jesus Christ in order to understand it from a social media and technology perspective.

SPIRITUAL AUTHORITY

'All authority has been given to Me in heaven and on earth. Go therefore...'

Before asking us to go, Jesus begins this verse by talking about the type of authority that has been given to him: absolute authority over all things in heaven and earth.

'All authority has been given to Me in heaven and on earth. Go therefore...'

The word 'therefore' here is significant. Jesus wants us to go into this world and start fulfilling the Great Commission because he has been given all the authority. We know that just after this statement Jesus left the earth and went to be seated on the right hand of the father in heaven, so he was not just talking about his authority here, but rather the authority that we have been given and that we possess in and through him. As Christians, we all live in and through Jesus Christ, and when we do that, we have access to the same authority that he has. When we go about our work with the understanding of that spiritual authority, then we are not intimidated by the things we don't understand. We operate from a position of authority and make use of all things in this world to fulfil the Great Commission.

Sometimes you may look at all the technological advancements in the world and wonder (and even fear) if you'll be able to handle all of it. You may look at the ever-growing list of new social networks, new types of content, new media, new technology and all the new gadgets and feel lost, left behind and ready to give up. But do not lose hope, and remember your God-given authority. The authority that God gives us in this scripture is 'all authority', which includes authority over social media, technology, internet, gadgets, electronic media and everything else. Even in the beginning, God wanted us to have dominion over all of these things (Genesis 1:26); we lost that dominion because of the fall, and Jesus Christ came and restored us into that place of authority and dominion. So do not be overwhelmed. You have the power and authority to dominate technology and social media.

You need not understand everything about a particular technology in order to put it to use. You just have to have a basic understanding of its application and impact. For example, in a church, the senior management team need not understand all the technical details of all the social media channels that they use. But they do need to understand their God-given spiritual authority over a tool like social media in order to engage, employ and delegate the right team to make full use of it.

REACHING NATIONS

When Jesus made this statement asking the disciples to go to all the nations, the transportation system was not sophisticated or evolved, and it

'Go therefore...'

took months to get from one nation to another. History tells us that the 12 disciples could cover only certain geographic areas in their limited lifetimes. So we know that Jesus was not making this statement only to a group of men who were standing in front of him; he knew those 12 men could only reach certain geographies, and he made that statement with the Church, the group of believers who would come later, in mind.

Today, with social media and technology, we can go to any place without actually being there in person. Churches and ministers can preach in one location and deliver that message to other nations using technologies like video or audio streaming and live video on social media. Older technologies like television and radio needed a lot of expensive infrastructure like satellites, cameras, broadcasting equipment and editing, but today you can podcast, vlog, blog and livestream the Good News right from your smartphone, and people from all over the world can access it without leaving the comfort of their homes.

When I grew up, live TV was a phenomenon. I was in awe knowing that the game that I was watching on this little box in a small town was actually happening right at that moment, thousands of miles away in another part of the world. And it took millions of dollars and hundreds of technicians in top TV channels to make that live broadcast happen. Just 15 years ago, it would have been too expensive for a normal church to even consider broadcasting a service live. Today you can do it for very little with a smartphone camera and free tools like Facebook Live that reach billions of people around the world instantly. So, all you need to accomplish the 'go' part of the Great Commission is the knowledge of how to put modern broadcasting technologies and social media tools to use.

DISCIPLING

Discipleship is an ongoing activity that can help people move closer to God. It involves learning the principles of God, applying them in your daily life and being a testimony for God's love. It takes time, effort and consistent ministry to empower and equip this type of

'...and make disciples...'

disciple, and social media can be an efficient tool in that process.

For example, let us assume that you are a small growing church. Most of your church members may be working professionals who are busy during the week. Fostering discipleship in them can be a challenge if you meet them only for a few hours a week on Sundays. How much can you teach them in, say, 40 minutes once a week? You could organise more prayer groups and small groups, but will people be able to attend them? Travel, traffic and time are three big challenges that you have to overcome. And even if you are able to overcome these and assemble a group of people in a room, you can do that only so many times a week. If you have a really gracious, committed and patient congregation who can assemble three or even four times a week, that's a maximum of 10 hours with your congregation in an entire week. Do you think that's enough time to effectively teach, equip, empower, encourage and walk with them as disciples?

But if you're a church with a busy congregation and you combine technology and social media with church services and other in-person ministry, you can foster discipleship on an ongoing basis. You can take your church material and use it as a source of teaching, inspiration and encouragement to your church members all week long, any time of the day. It is a scalable activity that does not depend on your involvement and time. For example, you can preach a sermon on Sunday and reinforce that sermon content all week long with a series of social media posts. Or you can choose a discipleship theme for the month, like servant leadership, and send out social media posts all month related to that subject, thus ministering to your congregation in that area.

Later in this book, I discuss strategies and techniques to make this process a reality in your ministry, helping you fulfil the discipleship part of the Great Commission effectively.

TEACHING

Discipleship can happen only with teaching. In my opinion, sometimes we fail to consider teaching as the primary element of modern Christian ministry. We focus too much on the activities, community and socialising parts of ministry that teaching

'...teaching them to observe all things that I have commanded you...'

starts to take a backseat. When we don't teach the Bible in depth, people don't understand the principles of God, and without those principles the doors are open for confusion of ideas and dilution of values.

Social media enables teaching ministry in the following ways:

- **Consistent delivery:** You can take a specific subject and deliver the teaching material consistently on social media over a long period of time. Unlike on TV or radio where you have a limited amount of hours, social media is your own broadcasting station and you can take as long as you like to deliver your teaching material. You can pace it without any external pressure.

- **Interactivity:** Social media is all about comments, feedback and inputs flowing in both directions. Almost all the platforms allow free flow of communication, creating a highly interactive teaching experience. Your audience can ask questions, express their opinions and share their expertise on the subject. In a Bible context, usually God gives different revelations to different people based on their situation and personal walk with him, so teaching on social media enables sharing of such valuable experiences, which can strengthen the body of Christ in unique ways.

- **Everyday context:** Teaching on social media is very different compared to traditional teaching in a room. When you teach in a particular location, the audience comes with a specific mindset. They shut out all other thoughts and focus on the teaching, which is a good thing. But when you are able to teach while people are at work or taking care of their everyday tasks, the teaching becomes more relevant and appealing because of the context. For example, suppose a person listens to your teaching on the subject of forgiveness during his lunch break at work when he's just had a fight with his colleague. The teaching comes alive and takes on a whole new dimension. It becomes a reality due to the context. This is possible only when we use technology and social media as a platform for teaching.

- **Empowered to share:** Today many believers face questions from their friends, family and colleagues concerning their faith. If your congregation has easy access to teaching material or can chat with elders or pastors on mobile devices, then they're able to answer questions and minister to others. For example, consider a working professional who is serious about living a Christian life. Her colleagues know this about her, and during a coffee break they ask her questions about the relevance of the Bible and what it says about marriage and family. This can be a great opportunity for the Christian woman to lead her colleagues to the truth if she has access to your teaching material on her mobile phone or if she can quickly connect with elders or pastors in your church on social media to ask them for the answers to tough questions. She's empowered to minister to her colleagues during their time of need because she has the information she needs at her fingertips. These little conversations with the right answers are the ones that make a big difference in building the Kingdom.

BEING IN GOD'S PRESENCE

Finally, Jesus encourages us by saying that he is with us always in these end times. We are not alone, and this is not a

'...I am with you always, even to the end of the age'

lonely journey. He is with us, and he will walk with us until the end. The fact that you are holding this book is proof that God wants you to start working on social media for your ministry. You could be reading a million other books, but you are spending time reading this one because God is ready to walk with you and help you use this tool to minister to others.

Personally I feel the power of this statement when I think about how this book came to be. The fact that you are reading this book is a miracle. The fact that I was chosen to write it is a miracle. When I had the leading to write a book like this, I was filled with doubt and a million questions. But look what happened. And it would have never happened if this statement 'I am with you always' was not true.

And when God is with us who or what can be against us? He can make the impossible happen. When God is with you, you can rest assured that he will help you use social media effectively as a tool to build his Kingdom of love. You may not understand everything about technology and social media, and you may not have all the answers, but have faith. Read this book with patience and apply each strategy that I will share in the following chapters prayerfully in your ministry. Because of God's empowering presence that is with you always, you will start seeing greater impact in the days to come.

SECTION 2

THE COMMUNICATION MODEL

CHAPTER 4

THE CONNECTED CHURCH COMMUNICATION MODEL™

After Jesus' resurrection and ascension, the small group he left behind to continue his mission started expanding under the guidance and leadership of the disciples. There is a lot we can learn from this small group. For a new movement, they recorded a tremendous growth rate. For example, when Peter preached one time, he saw 3,000 followers added to the group on that single day. Though the growth was mainly because of the power of God working in their midst, it also had much to do with the way the disciples operated. The Book of Acts recorded both the theological and the operational details of the early Church so that we can learn from it.

LEARNING FROM THE EARLY CHURCH

When we take a closer look at how the disciples operated, it reveals a pattern:

- They got together often and stayed connected most of the time.
- They worshipped together in one accord.
- They broke bread together and shared their meals often.
- They ministered to people together (and ministered to each other).
- They shared their worldly possessions with one another.
- Whenever they were together (which was most of the time), the Holy Spirit worked mightily among them with signs and wonders.

Do you see a pattern of togetherness and being connected?

The early Church was a *Connected Church.*

The Church worked and operated as one body with one mind, one goal, one God, one spirit and one purpose.

I call this a *connected state.*

In this connected state, the early Church was able to function as one, communicating seamlessly with each other irrespective of their differences. This state helped them create a big Kingdom impact in their society. They were able to thrive in the midst of persecution by the mighty Roman Empire and pierce the mindsets and strongholds in their own community and other surrounding communities, adding great numbers to the Church.

Because the early Church operated in a connected state, the Holy Spirit and the power of God could work easily and mightily through them. Many miracles and divine interventions are recorded in the Book of Acts – the lame walked, the blind saw, prison gates opened up miraculously and the dead rose again. When things like this happened it was not easy for the outside world to ignore them, heads turned in amazement and people started noticing the power of this movement. But it was not magic, it was simply God's love at work and the oneness of the Church that enabled such miracles. Now in the 21st century, we can also experience the same power if we learn to operate as a *Connected Church*.

Unfortunately today we as the Church have started operating as individual islands and segregated groups. We have created, invented and established many divisions, organisations, denominations, rules, orders, methods, regulations, structures and procedures that make it a serious challenge to stay connected as one body.

You may argue, 'But the early Church was a *small* group. So they were able to stay together, communicate easily, sort out differences and remain connected. Today we have grown in numbers. We, the people who declare Jesus Christ as our Lord and Saviour, are millions spread all around the world in different nations, with different languages and cultural backgrounds. Is it practically possible for today's Church to stay connected and operate as one body?'

Yes.

The Connected Church Communication Model™ that I outline in this chapter and the S.P.I.R.I.T. Framework™ that we will discuss later in the book are a small part of a big answer to that important question.

COMMUNICATION – THE KEY TO CONNECTIVITY

God designed us to be communicators. Communication is the foundation of *connectivity* in any relationship, organisation and even family. The more we communicate, the better are our chances of staying connected. That is why marriage counsellors advise couples to take time to communicate with each other to resolve conflicts.

We as human beings are constantly communicating to one another. In schools and colleges, we use teaching as a means of communicating knowledge. In businesses, we use meetings and conference as a means of communicating ideas. In marketing and advertising, we use text and visuals as a means of communicating a benefit or a value of products and services. Communication is an important invisible glue that keeps our society together and our everyday life going.

The same is true for the Church. Communication is the key to keeping the Body of Christ connected. The creation was designed by God to enable communications. Right from the Garden of Eden we see God placing great importance on keeping the communication channels open between Him and man. We see God walking with man in the cool of the day, probably discussing plans and strategies he had for his creation. We see Adam and Eve communicating with each other constantly, so much so that Eve couldn't stop talking about the forbidden fruit to Adam.

But after the fall, one of the first things that happened was the disruption in communication between God and man, as man was cut off from God's holy presence because of sin. The communication between Adam and Eve also changed drastically after the fall. Before the fall, when Adam looked at Eve his words were 'bone of my bones and flesh of my flesh'[1], but after the fall he is seen saying 'this woman you gave me'[2]. Interpersonal communications seem to have undergone a transformation (for worse) after the fall.

Today we are redeemed.

Jesus came and restored our communications with God. Through what happened on the Cross, we are able to put away all that kept us away from God and freely communicate with God. And this freedom to communicate with God restores our ability to have meaningful interpersonal communication with each other too.

So even as a Church we are able to communicate in a restored redeemed state. Church communications primarily happen in two settings: One within the Body of Christ and the other outside the Body of Christ. The former is for edification, building and supporting, while the latter is for proclamation, helping and sharing.

THE NEED FOR A COMMUNICATION PLATFORM

In order to communicate freely both within and outside the Church we need a common platform and an environment for communication. The platform or the environment must fulfil the following criteria:

- Help members of the Church search, find and locate one another when required
- Help us stay connected on demand, whenever we need one another
- Give us flexibility to choose the depth in the connection, such as connecting closely with some while simply staying in touch with others
- Help each of us express our unique gifts, talents and calling to one another
- Help us express and display our God-given knowledge, expertise, thoughts and plans so that we might help one another
- Help us learn from each other
- Help us know how to pray for one another
- Help us communicate without being limited by distance, location and space
- Help us communicate without being limited by the number of people the platform can hold

- Help us communicate without being limited by cost and economic factors

The early Church probably had access to such an environment because it was small in size and they were not spread too far from each other geographically. But one of the challenges that has kept today's Church from achieving close connectivity is the lack of such a common platform that could connect the entire Church irrespective of denominations, differences and practices.

AND... LET THERE BE SOCIAL MEDIA!

Now we have social media that can fulfil almost all of the criteria above. It can be the tool that meets the two important needs of the Church today:

1. Need for a platform to communicate and minister to each other within the Church
2. Need for a platform to communicate, serve and minister to people who need help and are yet to hear the good news about the love of God, outside the Church

In fact, the Church has never had such a barrier-free communication capability. Innovations in technology can make us more effective in ministry today than our predecessors. Before he left, Jesus said, 'You will do greater things than I did', and I believe technology and social media were some of the things he had in mind when he made that statement.

The important thing to note with social media is that most of us are already on this platform. We all use social media in some form or the other. With low-cost smartphones and increasing global connectivity, social media channels are getting bigger each year as more people sign up as users. At the time of writing this book, Facebook has more than 1.7 billion monthly active users[3]. Between Facebook and four other top social media networks, a good majority of the Church and the audience that needs to hear the good news are already connected on one common platform.

As a Church if all of us work towards integrating this platform in our regular communications, the possibilities are limitless:

- Anyone can tap into the resource and knowledge pool that God has placed within the Church easily, with just a few clicks.
- Anyone who needs help will be able to reach out to others.
- Anyone who needs prayers will be able to reach out to others.
- We can have a free flow of wisdom, revelation, information, resources and knowledge, enabling the Holy Spirit to empower us in unique ways.

The need for the Church to operate with such efficiency using technology, social media and other digital tools is significant in these end times.

THE CONNECTED CHURCH COMMUNICATION MODEL™

Though social media is a powerful tool, it can be complicated, distracting, time consuming and overwhelming if you do not have a structured approach to it. I have seen many individuals and organisations jump into social media enthusiastically without doing their homework, only to realise that they are unable to see tangible results or impact even after investing significant time, energy and resources.

The main objective of this book is to give you this structured approach.

Such an approach will not only help you but it will also help your audience as they are ministered to in a more meaningful way. And over time, as ministries around the world adopt such a structured approach to social media, the Church will find itself serving and meeting people's needs more efficiently. This will also mean that as a Church the entire Body of Christ can stay connected with each other using a common platform like social media, encouraging, edifying and helping each other. As we discussed earlier, this connected state of the Church will increase its effectiveness manifold. That is my hope and prayer.

In this chapter, I will take you through the four components of The Connected Church Communications Model™. Following that, in the next six chapters, we will look at the six-step S.P.I.R.I.T. Framework™ that is designed to help you implement this communication model into your ministry. As you (and your team) work your way through the next seven chapters, you should have an actionable strategy for your social media ministry. Let's get started.

The four components of The Connected Church Communications Model™ are:

1. The Core
2. The Community
3. The Content
4. The Channel

The first two components determine the *direction* of your social media ministry, and the next two components determine the *impact and effectiveness* of your social media ministry.

Component 1: The Core

The core is the WHY of your social media ministry.

It is the central piece and the reason you are going to do what you are planning to do on social media. The core component consists of a set of purpose statements that define the mission of your social media ministry.

Here is a set of questions that will help you figure out the purpose:

- Why do you want to use social media for your ministry? What is the purpose?
- Is the purpose of your social media ministry aligned with your overall life purpose or organisational calling? If so, how?
- In what way do you think social media can help you better minister to your audience?
- Why is this step important for your ministry right now? How does this impact your current plans? How does this impact your future plans?

- Is this something God wants you to focus on and prioritise right now in your ministry? If so why do you think he wants you to do this?
- After one year of social media efforts, what is the change you expect to see in your ministry? What kind of outcome do you expect? (Answer the same question for a three-year and five-year period.)

These are some of the questions that can help you get clarity and answer the question 'Why am I doing this?'. Add more details as you see fit. You may not have all answers right now, but answer as many questions as you can with as much detail as possible. You can always revisit these answers to add, delete and make modifications.

Articulating and capturing your thoughts prayerfully at this early stage can help you trace your path back to the original purpose in case you get lost on the way. Keep them simple, don't use complicated sentences or abbreviations that you may not recollect after a couple of years.

Get the help and suggestions of a mentor or trusted employees or friends and family while filling out the questions in this chapter. Ask them to help you answer these questions based on their knowledge of you and their own experience.

Store these answers in an accessible place. You could write them in a journal/planner, print them out as posters or keep them in an electronic form. But make sure you keep them in a place that is accessible so that you can use them to constantly remind yourself why you are doing what you are doing and course-correct when necessary. These statements are like the coordinates of a map that will guide you to your final destination. We will use these answers later in the book as a foundation for further planning.

Component 2: The Community

The community is the WHO of your social media ministry.

Create a list of people, groups, organisations and the entities who will benefit from what you are going to do on social media. In business terms, think of this as your target market or target audience that you will be ministering to.

This is an important step because later when you work on listing the things you want to do on social media, you will be faced with a lot of questions – What type of content to create? What should be the frequency of your social media posts? What channels to use? How to design your visual elements? What tone and type of language should you use? and so on. The answers to many of these questions will depend on your definition of the community. When you know your community, you know what will be relevant to them and make decisions based on that knowledge.

Existing community - If you are a church or ministry that has been in operation for a few years, you probably have an established community. Now you need to define it from a social media perspective. For example, if you're a youth ministry, you know who you are ministering to, but do you know your audience from a social media perspective? Do you know their behaviour on social media? Do you know their preferences on social media? Do you know how they spend their time on social media? These are some of the things you need to think about.

Extended community - Think about the people who are connected to your existing audience. For example, in your youth group your audience has a network of friends, classmates and colleagues on social media. So when people in your youth group LIKE, SHARE and COMMENT on your social media posts, it is going to be visible to their network. That is how all social media channels are designed to function. This means the extended network (friends of followers) also become part of your community. So, the social media community that you will be ministering to could be much bigger than the community that you see and know.

Identifying your community

If you are new to ministry or an individual still figuring out who your community is, apart from thinking about the audience that you might be comfortable with, take time to look inside of you and see if God has placed a burden in your heart for a certain group of people. It may be connected with your own personal testimony or story. Maybe God helped you overcome something so that you can help others. Blessed to be a blessing. For example, as a young man, I was in an impossible debt situation. God helped me overcome my debt. During that period, I felt a great burden to help other people who were going through a debt crisis. So, 'people in debt' became my community for a season in my life. I started thinking about them, creating written material, presentations, and organising conferences for them. Right now my community is 'the Church – ministries, churches, missionaries and believers in the marketplace who need help with social media'. That is where my heart is at this season. So I plan all my current social media activities around this community. Think about your community – the group of people that you want to minister to on social media at this season of your life.

Here are some ways to profile and define your community:

- **Geographic profile** – People in certain country, city, location, climate, culture, etc.
- **Demographic profile** – Age, gender, family size, income, occupation, education, marital status, etc.

- **Psychographic profile** – Attitudes, beliefs, faith, habits, status factors, visual appeal, spending patterns, etc.
- **Behavioural profile** – How they spend time, what content they consume, what their habits are, what their preferences are, etc.

Tip: Keep your core purpose statements in front of you while you think about the community profile that you want to build and serve using social media.

Component 3: The Content

The content is the WHAT of your social media ministry.

Content is the way in which you express or convey your core message to your community. There are 3 primary types of content that are used to express a message on social media:

- **Spoken content** – Created in church services, seminars, conferences, events, studio recordings, radio shows, podcasts, etc.

- **Written content** – Created for books, blogs, research papers, magazines, etc.
- **Graphical visual content** – Created as images, designs, memes, infographics, slides, videos, animations, etc.

Having clarity on the content component can help you with the foundational decisions you will need to make in social media ministry. In a nonprofit that I know, the primary content creator was more comfortable with writing than with speaking. So my suggestion to them was to design the entire online campaign calendar and workflow primarily based on the written content instead of videos or images. They still have to work on videos and images to fulfil other marketing requirements from a social media angle, but the workflow strategy took a different route based on the 'content-creation comfort zone' of the primary content creator.

We will go deep into the content subject in Chapter 7 of the book when we talk about packaging. Right now think about the following and document your thoughts:

- **Content type that you prefer:** The type of content that you are most comfortable creating (you can have more than one and prioritize them)
- **Content type that will help you fulfil your purpose:** Look at the purpose statement that you wrote earlier in the core component section of this chapter. Now think about the type of content that will help you fulfil that purpose. For example, if your purpose is to research a specific topic and spread awareness about it, you may

decide to have written content as your primary type of content along with some videos and podcasts as the secondary type of content.

- **Content type that is preferred by your community:** Look at the community that you are going to serve and think about the type of content that they might prefer. This might be different from the type of content that you are comfortable with.

Component 4: The Channel

The channel is the HOW of your social media ministry.

Think of the channel component as the vehicle through which you share your content to your community. This is a dynamic element that will keep changing based on the evolution of technology. Key innovations and disruptive companies will determine the channels that have the most reach.

There are no right and wrong selections when it comes to channels. The most effective communication channel for your ministry is the one in which your audience spends time. If they prefer Facebook and spend time on Facebook, then that is where you should be. It becomes your primary channel. Tomorrow, if they move to some other channel, then you will move too. That is how channels work. It is your primary responsibility to track their preference and change your communication strategy accordingly.

Here is a list of questions to help you gain clarity on the channel component:

1. What is the social media channel(s) that your community uses the most? The one where they spend most of their time?
2. How does your community consume their daily news? TV, radio, social media, etc.
3. What are the channels that are most suited for the content types that you plan to use for reaching your community?
4. Currently where is your online traffic coming from? Which social media channels gives you the maximum return on investment for your efforts, time and money (if you are placing ads) right now?

If you are not sure of the answers to these questions (or questions in the earlier sections), you could conduct a survey among your audience or community. It might be a simple one-to-one chat, a formal letter-based survey or an online survey. Ask them for answers to the questions that you are not sure of. If you are a church, you can invite your church members to spend a few minutes after the church service filling out a survey form. Do not ask more than 10 questions in the survey, and it should not take more than 5 minutes to complete. Ask as many objective type questions as possible to make it easier for them to answer.

Congratulations! Now you have the components of the communication model in place. This will help you steer your social media ministry in the right direction.

In the next six chapters we will go through the six-step S.P.I.R.I.T. Framework™ that will help you implement this communication model in your organisation or ministry. As I mentioned earlier, don't worry if you do not have all the answers now. As you go through the framework and as we dive deeper into practical steps, you will start getting clarity on the four components of the model. You can always come back and revisit these elements.

It is perfectly fine to spend a lot of time getting through this chapter, documenting your thoughts, conducting a survey, getting inputs from others, praying about it, etc. This is the most important chapter in the book, and these four components will be the key long-term drivers of your social media ministry. It is good to take time to work on them.

———～———

To access additional resources, tools and information related to this chapter, visit
www.theconnectedchurch.org/tccbook/chapter4

SECTION 3

THE FRAMEWORK FOR IMPLEMENTING THE COMMUNICATION MODEL

CHAPTER 5

AN INTRODUCTION TO THE S.P.I.R.I.T. FRAMEWORK™

A framework makes it easier to implement a model or a process and provides a point of reference for you to return to at any stage of implementation. The S.P.I.R.I.T. Framework™ is designed to help you implement and integrate social media communications into your ministry.

In my early years as a social media consultant I did not have a framework or a structure. I was all over the place, trying to do various tasks as the need arose. I went after every shiny red ball that surfaced on the social media scene and wasted a lot of time. I found that most strategies that I implemented and campaigns that I ran worked well for a while in isolation, but since I did not integrate my efforts I was unable to see long-term results. I was dreaming big and building tall towers without a strong foundation.

But as time went by, I realised the need for a structured approach to social media communications (thankfully). I saw a pattern in what was working and what was not. I documented the sequence in which things worked well. And whenever I worked on social media campaigns in a structured, sequential manner, I saw long-term, sustainable and scalable results. I soon realised that if I developed and documented my approach then any ministry would be able to replicate my results by following a simple, step-by-step framework. The S.P.I.R.I.T. Framework™ is a result of that documentation.

The benefit of working on this framework will be evident not only in your online ministry but also in the overall growth of your organisation. Some of what you will implement will help you streamline your everyday organisational workflow. For example, the *structuring* step is almost like a mini-organisational restructuring that will help you rethink the way your ministry operates.

The S.P.I.R.I.T. Framework™ will ensure that you do things in the right sequence and that you do not miss any key foundational elements before you proceed to the advanced levels. As I walk you through each step, by the end you will see the 4 components of The Connected Church Communication Model™ working in your ministry and you will have a strong foundation on which you can build as high a building as you would like. If you are working with your team, I recommend implementing each step along with them, discussing key points and answering the questions provided at the end of each step.

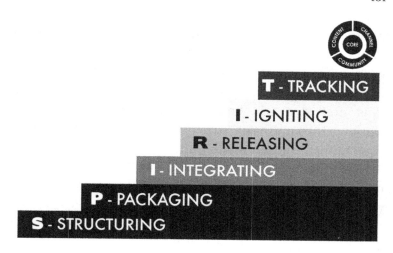

There are six steps in the S.P.I.R.I.T. Framework™, and you should work on them in the order presented here. You can always come back to any part and add more details to it, but it is best to progress in order because they build on each other.

#1 - STRUCTURING

While it is tempting to start your social media ministry by posting something on Facebook or Twitter, that is not the ideal way to start. Would you release a newspaper advertisement for your organisation, spending a lot of money, without thinking about what you will do when the responses come in? Or without thinking about whether your organisation has the capacity to deal with the results of the advertisement? You would not. You should think about social media promotions in the same way. It is also a 'medium' and a very powerful one at that. Just because it is a free or low-cost medium does not mean you should use it unprepared. Prepare for it just as much as (or maybe even more than) you would for a traditional media. You need a firm structure, like the skeleton that supports your body, before you start your social media efforts. This first step will help you build that skeleton by working through basic structuring (or restructuring) of your ministry goals, making them relevant to the social media audience. Then we discuss how to structure your ministry team, your teaching material, your resources, your presence and more.

#2 - PACKAGING

In this step, you learn how to package your ministry resources and material into various formats that can be used in social media. We discuss various ways of packaging content – written, audio, video, visual – and how each of them can impact your social media ministry. You also learn how to package your existing content and prepare your ministry to package content in the future.

#3 - INTEGRATING

In this step, you figure out how to integrate social media into every part of your ministry. Social media is not a standalone department. It should become part of everything that you do. We look at how you can infuse social media into regular ministry activities like church services, intercessory prayer meeting, worship services, Sunday school, special events and more. You also learn about ways of integrating your offline promotions and advertising activities with social media.

#4 - RELEASING

This step addresses how to release your packaged social media content in various channels. Random social media posts will not produce results. You need to have a strategy for every piece of content you post. This step will give you clarity on your internal social media workflow.

#5 - IGNITING

In this step, you learn how the content you post on social media can be ignited to ensure that it reaches the right audience. Social media space is getting more and more crowded every day with millions of blogs, videos and other content being posted. How will your ministry content overpower all the other content and stand out in this crowded space? This step helps you amplify and ignite your content to overcome the surrounding distractions.

#6 - TRACKING

Social media is a space that is always changing and transforming. This final step of the S.P.I.R.I.T. Framework™ focuses on practical ways to track and measure all your social media activities. Tracking helps you understand what works and what does not so that you can alter your approach accordingly.

At the end of this section of the book, you should be well prepared and poised to start your social media ministry journey, using it to build God's Kingdom.

Let us get started!

CHAPTER 6

THE S.P.I.R.I.T. FRAMEWORK™ - STRUCTURING

The skeletal system of the human body was designed by God not only to give us a shape but also to hold vital organs in place for efficient functioning. In this first step of the S.P.I.R.I.T. Framework™, you will learn how to do something similar for your social media efforts by creating a framework that will hold the various components of your social media ministry together. Structuring your social media activities can help you get good results by bringing clarity and efficiency into the workflow. This step requires you to examine your current operations and may warrant modifications at the foundational level.

SOWING BEFORE REAPING

I run a digital marketing agency[1] that helps startups, businesses, nonprofits and churches with their digital marketing needs. Sometimes when we get enquiries asking our agency to help with social media, the prospects quote the work we have done with another client and tell us, 'We want to see the same results that you have produced for this particular organisation. And we want it now!'. We patiently explain to them that all the outcome they see for that client – the social media following, the high level of engagement, the high level of reach and more – is the result of many months of hard work preparing, structuring, restructuring and laying the foundation. Good external results invariably have a strong internal foundation. Social media success is not magic or luck, it is hard work. And it takes time. Like any good endeavour, for social media success you have to set aside time for sowing if you expect to see a time of reaping.

The structuring that we discuss in this chapter is one such foundational preparatory step. Structuring time is the sowing time in your social media ministry. So work on it patiently. Try to overcome the temptation to jump onto Facebook and Twitter and start posting. That stage will come soon. First you need to work on some basic steps. You need to prepare your goals, your team, your presence and your material before you start your social media campaigns.

Without the proper structuring, even the most clever and creative promotional activities on social media may not produce desired results. For example, suppose that you are trying to get people to register for a ministry event by running promotional campaigns on social media. You work hard and create a great campaign, but if you do not make sure your website's registration page works well or if the website is unable to handle a high volume of traffic, the site may crash when your audience visits, and the effort of finding your audience on social media and bringing them to your website will be unfruitful. Similarly if you do not structure and prepare your team internally, you will not be able to run social media campaigns effectively because it takes a team to succeed on social media. That is why working on this part of the framework is important and a crucial first step for your social media ministry.

STRUCTURING YOUR GOALS

Note: This section suggests a basic goal setting format for nonprofit organisations that may not have started structuring their goals. If you are an established organisation with well-defined measurable goals or an individual in ministry with clear goals and KPIs, please feel free to use your existing format and skip this section. But do skim through the section and ensure that you have all the elements mentioned in this chapter because approaching goal setting from a social media perspective is slightly different than approaching it from a regular management perspective.

In Chapter 4, we talked about your *core* purpose statement and the *community* that you want to serve using social media ministry. Now let us build on that foundation by adding more details to those two components of The Connected Church Communication Model™. Create a document with a table (a spreadsheet in a computer or on a chart) which will be your structured goal sheet.

As shown in the sample image below, write down the core purpose statement on top as the main guideline for goal setting.

Column 1 – Use the community details as the main reference column. You can add more than one community to this column.

Column 2 – In this column, write down specific goals for each community. Your communications goals will include specific outcome you expect with respect to each community. Document your goals for a specific time period (6 or 12 months). You can have multiple goals for each type of community.

For example, if you serve as the youth minister in your organisation your goals might be:

- Increase youth ministry memberships
- Increase the involvement of the members in the ministry
- Improve knowledge about the Bible among the church youth

Columns 3 – List the activities or events that will help you achieve these goals.

Column 4 – Write down a goal description, this is a statement that combines the goal with an activity or an event listed in column 3. In this step try to quantify the goal by adding a measurable unit like a percentage or a number to each statement.

For example:

- Increase youth ministry's attendance by 10% by conducting a music concert for the youth so that they can bring their friends and family and introduce the ministry to them.
- Increase youth involvement in the ministry by 20% by organising camping trips for the existing youth members.
- Improve knowledge about the Bible among the church youth by conducting 2 teaching programs on 5 topics (be specific about the topic) and conducting a written or online quiz to measure the retention and comprehension.

Note the percentage numbers that I have included in the first two statements. All the goals that you set need to be specific and quantified. They need to be SMART goals – Specific, Measurable, Action-oriented, Realistic and Time-bound.

Column 5 – Against each goal statement in the list write down how you intend to measure whether the goal was achieved or not at the end of the specified time period. This is an important part of goal setting. In the business world, these are called KPIs – Key Performance Indicators. If you do not have a specific measuring system to know whether you are making progress or not, then goals will just be a set of statements on paper. In our youth ministry example, the KPIs would be:

- KPI for the effectiveness of the concert – The increase or decrease in the number of members enrolled in the youth church before and after the event.
- KPI for the effectiveness of the camping trip – The increase or decrease in the number of members involved in volunteering and leadership roles of the youth ministry before and after the event.
- KPI for the effectiveness of Bible teaching programs – Setting KPI for this activity is easy because you have a written or online assessment with the scores.

However there may be some activities which may not be directly measurable. For example, there may be spiritual elements like 'being more open to God's guidance' which cannot be measured in terms of numbers. You can leave the KPI section for those types of goals blank. But for a few exceptions, most of your activities should have some form of KPI that can be measured directly or indirectly. I strongly recommend you spend time thinking about the KPIs for each of your goals. This will help when we get to Chapter 11 and discuss measurement. But I am getting ahead of myself. Let us focus on the structuring for now.

CORE PURPOSE STATEMENT

_____

_____

COMMUNITIES	GOALS (FOR _ MONTHS)	EVENTS OR ACTIVITIES	GOAL DESCRIPTION	KPIs	DATE & TIME

Involving your team

After you prepare the first version of this structured goal sheet, call for a meeting with all the departments in your ministry. If you are an individual, arrange a meeting with a group of friends, family, mentors or trusted advisors. Discuss each goal and KPI with them. Get their inputs, opinions and ideas. Collective wisdom always helps. The Bible says[2] '...a man of understanding will get wise counsel'

When you discuss the goals with your departments, allow them to add their own departmental goals to this sheet. Create separate subsections of the sheet if you need to, but try to maintain a single document so that you have a single view of all the goals.

Matching goals with activities and setting timelines

Column 6 – Add timelines (dates and durations) to each goal. Assess the date by which you want to accomplish that goal and how long the goal will last, if it is time-specific. Ask all the team leaders or division coordinators to review the timelines for any departmental conflicts and resolve them.

Ideally you should create these goals for a period of at least one year, but break it down into smaller chunks such as half yearly, quarterly, monthly and weekly for ease of execution. Here are some practical tips to ensure you don't miss any important events:

- First look at all the regular known events – for churches it could be Good Friday, Easter, Christmas and New Year services.
- Select a goal that each of these fixed, known events would help you achieve. They may impact more than one goal; repeat them under every goal that they impact because the KPI might vary for each goal. For example, a church's New Year service might be relevant to the goal of increasing church memberships and the goal of reaching more people on social media. But each of those goals has a different KPI or unit of measure. Including the event in both goals will help you track how this single event contributed to two different goals.
- Similarly create a list of special events for each year and match it with the goals.

- Then look at the goals that are not well supported by events or activities and consider including a few more events. But do not try to add an activity or event if it's not the right fit. It is ok for a goal not to have many supporting events. Events are not the only way to achieve a goal. There are other ways like advertising, content marketing, etc. some of which we will discuss later in the book.

Now you have a document that gives you an overview of your long-term objective, a list of goals and supporting events and activities that can help you achieve your goals. After you develop this structured goal sheet document, place it in a common, visible location and refer to it whenever you need to. The goals that you created will help you determine what you want out of social media. As we move along and discuss various aspects of social media (like content, promotions and advertising) you will see how to achieve these goals with the help of social media.

STRUCTURING YOUR ORGANISATION AND TEAM

Social media ministry is like an airplane: It has many moving parts and needs the concerted effort of many departments working together in order to cruise smoothly. Now that you have your goals ready, let us look at how you can prepare your team to succeed in social media.

For individuals in ministry

If you are an individual in ministry – a missionary or a marketplace minister – you need to come up with a plan to accomplish your social media goals yourself. With a little bit of planning and organisation, you can be successful.

Here are some things for you to think about:

- How will you spend the limited time that is available each day to advance toward your social media goals?
- Can you use productivity apps, gadgets and software to help you be more efficient?
- Can you partner with other people to help you?
- Can you work with volunteers?
- Can you get help from freelancers, agencies or other ministries?

God designed us to be collaborators, and we function much better when we work with others. So I suggest you do not try to do everything by yourself. There are challenges associated with working with other human beings, and sometimes you would rather do things yourself, but working with complicated people and achieving great things together is better than not achieving anything by working alone. Be open to partnerships and collaborations.

For organisations in ministry

If you are a nonprofit organisation in ministry or a

church, your existing organisation and team needs to be structured to align with your social media goals.

The first step is to get all your team members aligned with the vision. Along with your core team, get other church leaders involved in this process and explain your vision for social media ministry. Address concerns and answer questions that they may have. Get them on board with the idea of getting into social media. Like any other good project, social media requires the coordinated efforts of multiple departments within your ministry.

Social media core team

Once all your team members understand the vision and get on board, you can gather a team that will be directly involved in the social media efforts. This will become the dedicated social media core team, and it will be supported by all other teams and departments. The way it will be structured is:

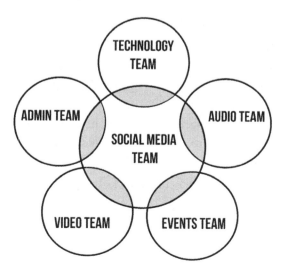

As you can see, the dedicated social media team will be supported by the other teams within the organisation. Social media requires tight integration of various departments to make it a success. For example, suppose you decide to make social live video streaming of church services on Facebook one of your main social media activities for your ministry. This decision will impact and involve the following departments and their operations:

- The events department has to provide a space for live streaming gadgets and devices.
- The video department has to deploy a director in the video mixer to ensure that the live audience doesn't see the floor or random footage.
- The preacher or speaker has to be aware that people are not just hearing him in person but they are also watching him from around the world using their mobile phones and desktops.
- The audio department has to ensure that the quality of the audio is good and there are no noises, distortions or variations in the volume levels.
- The technical department has to ensure that the internet bandwidth is ready to support all of this activity.
- The maintenance department has to ensure that there are no power surges and the required cabling for this new activity is in place.
- The support team needs to be prepared to answer calls and emails from people experiencing technical problems during the livestream.

It takes an army to wage a war, and we're at war in the spiritual online realm, fighting against spiritual darkness, principalities and powers that are trying to stop us from using social media to help people, lead them in the right direction, serve them, and save the lost. Prepare your army for social media warfare.

Social media team matrix

With multiple departments and people involved in your social media activities, it is a good idea to map all the roles and responsibilities. You could create a social media team matrix document (a spreadsheet) that maps all the team members, departments and talents required to accomplish your social media goals. For example, every month or every quarter you can use this team matrix document when meeting with all your department heads to plan the campaigns. The social media team can present their campaign plan from the structured goal sheet, and the other departments can look at which areas each of them needs to contribute and talk about any challenges they may have and resolve them. For example, the social media team may ask for extra internet bandwidth from the maintenance team for the next two months to carry out a special social media video campaign. The infrastructure/maintenance team needs to know about this request in advance so that they can plan and make the provision for it. This kind of clarity and collaboration will increase the effectiveness of your social media ministry.

Social media skills required

The social media team in your ministry requires many specialists to make it work.

- **The source content creator:** The key person or persons in your ministry who will preach, teach, advise and counsel people on a particular topic and create the source material for the ministry. This material could be in written format or spoken format – video or audio.

- **Social media strategist:** A team member who will use the source content to come up with social media marketing campaigns, strategies, ideas and innovative ways of presenting your core message. This person should have knowledge of current industry trends and stay on top of developments in social media marketing.

- **Project management team:** Team members who will convert the social media strategy into an actionable plan with tasks, calendars, campaigns, timelines and more, coordinating with the rest of the team on a regular basis to bring the plan to life and measuring impact on a regular basis. The project leader from this team could be the single point of contact and the coordinator for the entire social media effort of your ministry.

- **Content management team:** Team members who will take the original source content and work on it, customise it, package it, edit it and make it suitable for various social media channels.

- **Visual content production team:** Graphic designers and video editors who will work on the content and create visual elements to present the idea. Visual elements are vital for social media.
- **Social media management team:** Team members who will place the content and visual elements on various social media channels. This team will monitor all the social media accounts and engage with people on a regular basis, and it will also measure and track the progress of all the social media activities and report back to the rest of the team on what changes need to be made.

Getting access to a team

As a ministry, there are multiple ways for you to get access to all these team members with various skill sets.

- **Be a one-man army:** If you are a small church and you are the only person in the social media division, you can work on the roles and responsibilities listed above by yourself. Even though it looks like a lot of work (and it is), if you manage your time efficiently and use the right tools, you can handle it. But as you reach a stage where your ministry grows and you're unable to manage the workload, then you might have to think about getting help.
- **Recruit a team:** If you have the resources to do it, you could hire the team with the required skill sets given above and start the operations.

- **Hire a consultant:** If you already have a team and you need a bit of direction and focus, you can hire a social media consultant to help you put these systems in place, set up the tools, train the team and ensure that you are on your way to being efficient and successful in your social media ministry.

- **Hire an agency:** If you are not sure about handling all of this in-house, then you can hire an agency, partnering with people specialised in this niche activity. You can assign one coordinator from the ministry to be the point of contact, and allow the agency to handle all the activities. Any good agency will have experienced people on their team for each of the roles listed above. So, you get access to all the skill sets and since it is managed by someone else on a regular basis, you are freed up to focus on your ministry while they handle all the social media operations. You can get weekly and monthly reports from the agency in order to stay on top of the campaigns and activities.

STRUCTURING YOUR COMMUNICATION MATERIAL

If you are an established ministry, you probably have a lot of teaching material – books, magazines, videos and audio. And in the days to come you are only going to create more of it. Structuring your resource material is the act of collecting and organising it in an orderly manner. In the next chapter we will discuss how to package these materials, and if you do not collect and organise them first, you will not be able to package them efficiently.

As a consultant, one of the first things I do when I start working with a ministry is take stock of all their teaching resources. I ensure that they are organised, indexed and documented before we start anything else. Content is the basis of all that we do in social media, whether it's written content, images, videos, books, magazines or any other form. Knowing what kind of content you already have on hand will help you plan for the future and figure out what kind of content needs to be created. So, take stock and gather in one place all the source content that might be required to help you get your social media ministry up and running. You may be surprised at how much material you already have as you turn up old sermon recordings, something you wrote once when you had a little extra time, old copies of magazines, books, video recordings and so on.

Step 1 - Taking stock

If you are an organisation, ask the people who have been with your ministry for the longest period of time for their help in locating materials and compiling a list. If you are the main content creator, share your personal journal. If you are an individual, collect all the media (video, audio and written content) that you may already have on one hard drive or similar storage location.

Create a list of all your resources on the computer using a spreadsheet. If you create the list on paper, task someone with entering it into the computer before you move on to the next step. Creating this digital record will make it easier to organise and update the list as your project progresses.

Step 2 - Organising

After you take stock of the material, you can organise it into whatever order makes the most sense. For example, collect all the tapes of your ministry over the years and organise them by date, popularity, topic or event.

Step 3 - Optimising

Is all your source content optimised for social media? For example, all your recorded sermon tapes have to be converted to digital format in order to be used on social media. Your ministry photos, videos and other archived content also has to be digitised and optimised for social media.

As you convert your source content for use on social media, start naming and tagging your resources strategically. Many ministries make the mistake of not naming the digital versions of their resources properly in the initial stage. Then after a few years, with weekly sermons and ongoing activities piling up, the volume of badly named content increases to an unmanageable level, requiring a huge effort to bring them back to order. So, I highly recommend establishing a naming convention that suits your operations, such as <sermon

title>-<date>-<speaker name>. Also tag your content (if possible) when you optimise it.

Step 4 - Storage

After you optimise your source content, think about how you are going to store it. As you start working on social media and other online activities, you or your team will create multiple copies of the same file, storing different versions of it in different locations using different names. This can cause a lot of confusion, and if you are not careful, at one point you may not even be able to find the original version. Very quickly, your digital trash can will build up and overwhelm you. So, even as you start your social media ministry, think about how you are going to store photos, videos, design files and audio files. Think about where you will store the edited files and files that are in progress. Think about how long you need to store them. Think about archiving options for the long term. Think about backups. Always save a copy of the original source content before you start working on it. And always plan to have a 3-2-1 backup: Back up your data in 3 different, unrelated locations at all times. 2 of which need to be local but on different medium or devices and 1 copy should be offsite. Losing precious content can be frustrating and a big time-waster.

STRUCTURING YOUR ONLINE PRESENCE

The easiest way to understand *online presence* is to compare it with a physical ministry building such as a church building. If you are a church, your bricks-and-mortar church building is your offline presence, and your website will be your online presence.

Why is it important to have a good-looking, strong and functional online presence? The effectiveness of your social media activity is determined largely by the effectiveness of your online presence. Social media is only a promotional tool that will get the attention of your audience in the wide world of the internet and bring them to the figurative doorstep of your online building. Once they reach the doorstep, whether or not they come in and get ministered by you depends on how your online presence is built. If they see a nice-looking, inviting, useful and helpful place, they might decide to step in. Or they might bounce off! (In the SEO world, the term for the rate at which a visitor leaves a website is rightly called a *bounce rate*.)

The online presence of any ministry today primarily consists of the following items:

- The website(s)
- The mobile assets - either a mobile-optimised website or mobile apps
- Search optimisation - how you show up in results of various search engines
- Social media presence on various channels
- Type of content you have on all of the above

Online presence is not about you, it's about your audience

Many ministries that I have interacted with think of website and mobile apps as places where people come and get more information about them. Even though that is true to some extent, it's not the right approach if you want to grow your influence online. Keep the focus of your online presence more on the audience than on you. You can still showcase your work and ministry, but if the website, mobile app and social media are designed to serve the needs of your audience, then you will have more people visiting, using and benefitting from your online presence. For example, when I was working on redesigning one church's website, I suggested that we move the 'About Us' section to the end of the menu instead of the beginning where you usually find it. We decided to keep the resources like video, audio and books as the first set of items in the menu instead. Visitors could still find the 'About Us' section, but it was no longer the centre of the website. When you build your online presence, build it around your audience and their needs.

Creating a user-friendly experience

Successful online presence is all about the experience that people have when they visit your website or social media or mobile app. Think about that experience and how you can make that experience much more meaningful and fulfilling for your audience. Make things easy for them when they interact with your ministry online. For example, if people want to donate, don't make it hard to find the form. As the leader of the ministry, you understand what your audience wants, so even if you do not understand technology you can provide guidance to your design and technical team on how you would like to serve people. Then they can design your online presence based on your inputs.

To access additional resources, tools and information related to this chapter, visit
www.theconnectedchurch.org/tccbook/chapter6

CHAPTER 7

THE S.P.I.R.I.T. FRAMEWORK™ - PACKAGING

Content is the driving force behind social media. From a social media workflow perspective, there are two types of content: source and packaged. Source content is the original content that you as a content creator are comfortable creating; packaged content is the content that is born out of that source content. The packaged content is usually a set of various types of content packed in various formats, each for a specific social media promotional purpose and for the convenience of the audience.

SOURCE CONTENT

Original or *source content* captures the idea, message or information that the creator (an individual, organisation or entity) is trying to convey.

Every communication has a creator, whether it's a preacher, a speaker, a writer or a thought leader. The source content can be created by a single source or through collaboration. For example, a Sunday sermon by your senior pastor is content created from a single source, but a webinar in which you interview an expert from another ministry and a guest blog on your website are collaborative content. Both forms of original content are effective on social media.

The Bible is probably the most interesting piece of collaborative content ever: It has one main author, God, who passed on the original idea to human beings, and then 40 different authors collaborated over a period of 1,600 years to create one single piece of content!

CONTENT PACKAGING FOR SOCIAL MEDIA

Packaging is the art of taking a piece of your original source content and giving it a shape and form that is suitable for various audiences on various social media channels. There are two approaches to content packaging for social media. One is the *channel-based approach* where content is packaged based on the format, type, size or duration that is demanded by various social media channels. The second is the *purpose-based approach* where content is packaged based on the purpose for which it is created by the content creator. Both are effective approaches and they can be adopted in combination, based on the need. Each approach has three ways in which you can package the content.

Channel-based content packaging

1. **Reformatting:** *Reformatting* is creating different *formats* of the same *type* of content in order to suit different distribution channels and social media platforms. For example, you take *written* content, like a book, and *reformat* it for the Kindle platform, retaining the type of content (*written*). You reformat it only because the platform requires you to do so and because you like to make it suitable for the audience using that platform. In this approach, you do not alter the actual type of source content or the length or duration of the source content, like the number of words in a book or the number of minutes in a video or audio track; you simply reformat it. Here's another example: If your source content is video, then you retain the *type* of content as video but reformat it in 16:9 wide dimension for YouTube platform and in a 1:1 square dimension for Instagram.

2. **Resizing:** *Resizing* is creating different versions of the original content in various sizes. In this approach also you retain the type of content, and only change the size for a specific purpose. For example, you can take written source content like a book and resize it into several shorter blogs posts because of its suitability for social media promotions. You can further reduce the size of the content to create multiple social media posts for promotional purposes. So in this approach you resize the content by changing the length/duration while retaining its original type.

3. **Repurposing:** *Repurposing* is taking the original source content and converting it into a totally different *type* of content. For example, you take written content from a book and convert it into a video, audio, podcast, infographic and other popular formats. Repurposing is one of the most important approaches for you to consider because different audiences who interact with your ministry in the online space are primed to consume different types of content. Therefore, your ministry should be ready to present your content in a way that is appealing to and preferred by your audience. For example, let us assume you are a ministry that teaches married couples on marriage and family. And let us assume that your audience group consists of working professionals who have been married for 1 to 10 years. Apart from trying to make a family work, they are also trying hard to build their careers, so they have very little time to spare. Your strength is creating written content and not video content, so you write pages on family and post them on your blog. Do you think your audience will have the time to read all those blog posts? What they need is a set of short, two-minute videos with answers to specific marriage problems. Repurpose your written content into short videos to first grab their interest; what they see in the video must motivate them to spend more time on your blog, reading the more detailed written content posted there.

	REPURPOSING	RESIZING	REFORMATTING
FORMAT	☒	☒	✔
TYPE	✔	☒	☒
LENGTH / SIZE	☒	✔	☒

Purpose-based content packaging

In this approach you can package the content based on the purpose it serves for the audience. You must package the content in an *explanatory* long form if the audience needs that much explanation. But if they want summarised content that will save them time, then you must package it in *summarised* short form. But if you like to use the content for promotional purposes, then you must package it in the *promotional* form. Let us look at the three major types of original source content – written, video and audio – and consider how purpose-driven content packaging works for each of them

Explanatory packaging – Long-form content

Long-form content is good for and preferred by audiences who want to learn more about your ministry and who are researching a specific subject. For them, a few sentences or even a paragraph of content may not be enough. They want a whole book because they are keen to learn more and they see you as an authority on that subject.

Written content

Written content is the oldest and most prominent type of content. Despite developments in technology and the connected world with regard to video and audio formats becoming more popular, written content is still what drives the internet. For example, Google and other search engines provide search results based mostly on written words. So written content is important from a search engine optimisation perspective too.

Long-form packaging for written content can take the following forms:

- Books
- Detailed blog posts (more than 2000 words)
- Sermon transcripts
- Magazines
- Research papers
- Articles

Video content

Video is the fastest growing content format in the world. For a Christian organisation, producing video-based content used to involve a high cost and complicated logistics. But now video production has become simple thanks to smartphones, handheld cameras and other affordable gadgets that allow you to shoot videos in a few minutes and post them immediately on a variety of channels.

But please be aware of the quality of the videos you produce and share. When the quality of video and audio is high, people absorb the information better, making the content more far-reaching and more effective. People also feel more comfortable sharing high-quality information with their network because it gives them value as a thought leader.

Packaging video content in long form should be engaging, bearing in mind short attention spans. The following forms are well-suited for sharing educational content with a captive audience that signs up voluntarily:

- Streaming of live events and church services
- Archives of recorded messages from live events and services
- Studio recordings of specific messages
- Detailed online course videos on specific topics
- Webinar videos

Audio content

Audio has been well-suited to ministries and churches for many years, but now it has evolved into online mobile-driven content, with more people listening to online radio and podcasts through their mobile phones. You need to package your audio material for both on-demand and live consumption. Podcasting in particular has seen great growth in the last few years, and there are millions of people who listen to podcasts regularly because of the convenience it offers. Some of the long form audio content forms are:

- Audio streaming of live events and services

- Archives of recorded audio messages from live events and services
- Studio recordings of specific messages
- Podcasts
- Webinar recordings

Summarised packaging – Short-form content

Short, summarised content is becoming more popular given that people's attention spans are getting shorter and the amount of content is increasing exponentially. Short-form content delivers the essence of the message in less time, but creating it poses the challenge of expressing your ideas in just a few words or minutes as a video or audio file.

Written content

When summarising long-form content, make sure there is enough value for the audience. Use summarised content as a lead generator to get people to consume long-form content. Some example of summarised written content are:

- Blog posts
- Summary of a sermon or a teaching session
- eBooks and white papers
- Slide decks
- Detailed social media posts (500 to 1000 words)
- Website copy
- Editorials in magazines

Video content

These are shorter videos that summarise long-form video content. Try to use animations and other visual elements to help you convey the message and educate the audience in less time. Short-form videos are typically suitable for YouTube, Facebook and Live Video platforms. Some examples of short-form video content are:

- Video blogs with summaries
- Explanatory videos or promotional videos on a specific topic with animations
- Video versions of your podcasts
- Tutorial videos
- Step-by-step how-to videos
- Online course videos

Audio content

These are shorter audio content that summarise long-form audio content. This is helpful for people who want to listen to a short summary in situations like commute from work, just to get the essence of a message or information.

- Short summary of church sermons
- Short interviews and discussions
- Short testimonies and audio clips

Promotional packaging

You can also repackage long-form or short-form content created with the intention of promoting a particular message, event, product or a person. While the other types of packaging focus on adding value to the audience by giving as much information as possible, this type of packaging is deliberate in promoting something. This type of content addresses the values and benefits for the audience, but the central message will be promotional in nature.

Written content

Promotional packaging of written content has been used by the advertising industry for many generations, so it may be familiar to you. But when it is used in a social media context, much attention and care needs to be given to the device, audience and format.

- Descriptive content in social media posts
- Tweets
- Headlines
- Taglines
- Advertising copy
- Website copy on landing pages
- Advertorials in magazines

Video content

Keep the promotional videos short and simple with texts, graphics, statistics and few words. They can be used in all channels, especially in channels like Twitter and Instagram where there is a restriction for duration of video uploads.

- Short promotional videos of less than three minutes
- Video clips taken from a long sermon, exclusively for promotional purpose

- Infographic-style videos with motion graphics and animation
- Short, slide-based videos with benefits
- Brochure-style videos with event details and benefits

Audio content

This is similar to short commercials that we listen to on any radio show, but created for an online audience. In a few seconds you may need to summarise the value and benefit of whatever it is you are promoting.

- Short sample clips from sermons
- Radio ads
- Podcast ads
- Testimonies to promote an event or a product or a cause

INTERACTION STAGES VS TYPE OF CONTENT

The way the audience interacts and behaves in the online world is very different from the offline world. Consider these key aspects of the online audience behaviour when preparing your content:

- **They can be highly distracted.** You are not guaranteed a captive audience at all times. You need to package your content with this distraction factor in mind. For example, if a person walks into your church or ministry, once they are inside your premises there is not much distraction. They can focus on whatever you have to say or whatever you want them to do. But the online world is different. While they are browsing through your website and interacting with you, they have the freedom and the ability to simultaneously open another window or a tab on their device and access the resources of another website.

- **They have varying intentions.** The online audience has different intentions while interacting with you at different times. For example, when someone comes to your website or social media channel to look at your ministry address, even if you have the world's best sermon posted on the blog or on the top of the website, they will not look at it. They came for something specific, and they are focused only on finding it. They have a specific intent for each visit, and you need to package your content with their different intentions in mind.

- **They have varying amounts of time.** The online audience will spend hours on your social media or website one day and just a few seconds on another day. The amount of time that they spend each time depends on their intent and their preference. There is nothing you can do about it except make sure that you offer content in varying lengths that can accommodate any amount of time your audience has. Package your content with this time factor in mind.

- **They have a varying levels of interaction.** The online audience may choose to interact with you online in a formal, superficial, let-me-just-stay-in-touch type of way, or they may interact with you as someone who feels like they know you, almost like a friend or even family. In the friend and family levels, you have a deeper connection, meaningful comments, conversations, insights and opinions that can really matter. But because not everyone will bring this depth of interaction, you cannot have common, one-size-fits-all content for everyone. You need to plan and package your content to satisfy the various levels of interactions.

SOCIAL MEDIA AUDIENCE FUNNEL

One of the models that can help you get clarity on how to package your content for various situations, behaviours and scenarios is the *social media audience funnel*. The audience funnel is a proven model that has been used successfully by businesses in their sales and marketing departments. In social media, we use it with a bit of customisation. The top of the funnel represents the large number of people who will be exposed to your content on social media. Then, some of the audience will start becoming more interested in what you do and will get more involved with your content. They move to the next level of the funnel as they start interacting with you on a deeper level. As the funnel progresses, the interactions get deeper and more meaningful, but the total audience also becomes smaller and smaller. Finally you are left with only a fraction of the audience you started with at the top of the funnel, but they interact closely, communicate meaningfully, transact regularly, trust you completely, share your content widely and become a very precious audience who will stay with you for the long run.

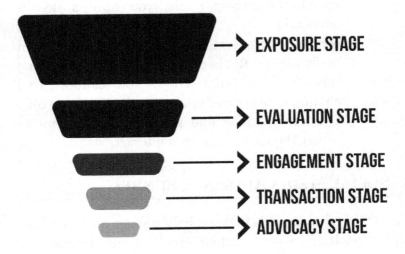

EXPOSURE STAGE

EVALUATION STAGE

ENGAGEMENT STAGE

TRANSACTION STAGE

ADVOCACY STAGE

Now let us look at each part of the funnel and see your audience's mindset and behaviour at each stage.

The Exposure Stage

At this stage of the funnel, the connected audience doesn't know much about you, so your key objective should be to give them as much information as possible. But keep in mind that the web is growing, and thanks to social media, people are bombarded with tons of content. They don't have all the time in the world to read your 100-page books and 30-minute sermons. The best way to engage with this audience is with short-form content -– snippets of your sermon in videos less than 2 or 3 minutes long, quotes from your sermon converted into graphic images, short blog posts (less than 200 or 300 words), short emails and the like.

The objective in this stage is to capture the attention of this audience. You can share the same short-form content from your social media channels available on the website or in your mobile app. Present a clear picture of your ministry in just a few seconds so that they don't have to spend hours trying to understand what your ministry is all about.

Thinking about search engine optimisation is crucial at this stage, because most of the audience at the top of the funnel will find your website, blog posts or social media channels from search engine results. For example, if you are in the marriage and family ministry, you might write a blog post on 'Ten ways to reduce fights in marriages'. When someone comes to Google and searches for the keyword 'How can I fight less with my wife', the search results will include your article, leading them to your blog page. When you give relevant content that ministers to this person and answers their question quickly, you have a good chance of moving them to the next part of the funnel.

The Evaluation Stage

In this stage, a portion of the total audience from the top of the funnel becomes more interested in your ministry and the type of content that they see on your social media channels. They start evaluating you. This is the stage where you give them as much information as possible in detail. With this audience in mind, you could prepare content about the values of your ministry, your beliefs, your vision, your mission, your plans, your strategy and how you would like them to be involved. This can be both long-form and short-form content. Since the audience is still in the top half of the funnel, I caution you about using too much long-form content. Some longer pieces are inevitable, but try to use as much short-form content as possible. Consider resizing your long-form into shorter versions. For example, instead of a 30-minute video on all the plans you have for your ministry, break it down into 10 three-minute videos, which are easier for the evaluating audience to consume.

The Engagement Stage

In the engagement stage of the funnel, your audience has started clicking, liking and commenting on your content. They have seen enough about you on your website or social media channels to know that they like you, and they have started engaging with you. The funnel gets a bit smaller in this stage because not everyone who comes across your content wants to interact or engage with you. So some of the audience ignores your content and moves on, but some will stay.

For the most part, the audience who has stayed with you in the engagement stage has done so not because they are being nice to you but because they find your content useful. Ministries that grow are those that offer value to the audience by giving them useful information. For the audience looking for value at this stage, you need not be so brief. Your content should be more detailed. But the keyword in this stage is 'value' and not 'length'.

Irrespective of the length of your content, at this stage you can provide immense value to the audience by sharing useful content that will make them feel blessed. Teach them, guide them, encourage them, thank them, ask them questions, give them opinions, share your expertise, give some freebies and make them happy. Reward them for their engagement. They will spend more time on your channels and websites consuming more content because they are eager to learn and they like what they have already seen. The longer you are able to keep them on your social media pages and website with your content, the better. This is the stage that determines how much lifetime involvement you will have with this audience. Reward them with free eBooks, gift coupons, webinars, podcasts and so on.

Also at this stage your audience is engaging with you by asking questions and commenting on your channels, so you need to be responsive. You should answer every question and reply to almost every comment – even the negative ones. If you do not respond to your engaged audience, there is a chance that you will lose them.

The Transaction Stage

Most organisations do a good job of finding and grabbing their audience until it comes to this part of the funnel. The funnel gets smaller, and the people at this stage are primed to start transacting with you and getting involved in a deeper level. They may be ready to start volunteering for church activities, signing up for seminars, buying your ministry products, giving donations and participating in your ministry at a deeper level. These are very valuable people. Think of them as your *online church members*. You need to minister to them, value them and help them the same way you would help and minister to your existing ministry or offline church members.

In fact, many of your existing ministry offline audience or church members may have become part of your online audience due to changes in circumstance such as relocation or travel, and their online behaviour will be similar to the rest of your offline church members. So any activity or preparation that you do online for your audience at this stage will also help your existing ministry members who have transformed into online members.

This is a good stage for you to consider creating exclusive communities or groups. You could open up a Facebook group only for this audience to share some special material and insights only with them. These are the people who would sign for a website membership or online subscription program if you have one.

In addition to being more detailed and potentially longer, the content you share with the audience at this stage should be personalised. For example, for everyone who buys a copy of your book online, you can send an email thanking them for their support (this is in addition to the automated email sent from your website) and sharing a few words of blessings. For anyone who signs up for a webinar, you could offer a special coupon code to use in your church webstore. You could also go a step further and organise a face-to-face event for all your online church members from one particular area. For example, if your church is in the US but you are visiting the UK for a conference, you could email your online members and ask them to meet you in a coffee shop. Or you might even organise a free speaking session in a hotel conference hall exclusively for them. At a small cost you are enriching and rewarding the people who have travelled three stages in the funnel and are making a special effort to stay connected to your ministry. They will appreciate this gesture, and it will also encourage some of them to move to the next, most important stage of the funnel.

The Advocacy Stage

This is the most important stage for any online (or even offline) audience. A small portion of your audience has become brand ambassadors for your ministry. They start talking about your ministry among their friends and family, and they introduce more people to your church website and ministry social media channels. They answer questions on social media on your behalf, they defend your doctrine and your belief system, they send emails to their personal contacts about your Sunday message and they post a Facebook status testifying how your sermons have touched them and helped them. They are valuable. This audience may be small in number, but they are the influencers who will help your ministry grow in the long run.

At this stage you need to provide tools to help your audience be advocates for you. On your website, make it easy for them to share your blog posts, and provide clear links for them to connect easily with all your social media channels. As in the previous stage, create personalised content for this audience and give them some very special privileges. Treat them like VIPs online, because that is exactly what they are. Sharing is the ultimate act of loyalty and trust. When your audience chooses to share your content with others, they are choosing to put their reputation in your hands. Create content that will reward them and keep them connected to you.

———————～———————

To access additional resources, tools and information related to this chapter, visit
www.theconnectedchurch.org/tccbook/chapter7

CHAPTER 8

THE S.P.I.R.I.T. FRAMEWORK™ – INTEGRATING

Social media is not a standalone activity. You may set up a separate social media department within your organisation, but the social media activity itself has to be part of all that you do in your ministry.

As I discuss in Chapter 1, the connected audience for your ministry is not always physically present in front of you, but they are connected with you all the time through social media. They wake up in the morning and open their social media channels, and they would be happy to see some news about what is happening with your ministry on that particular day. Social media is not just about posting a few updates about your sermons, special events and Sunday services. It is about keeping your connected audience informed of all your progress, your challenges, your victories and your life as a ministry. Being transparent and communicative on a regular basis will build great levels of trust with your connected audience, and they will truly feel connected with your ministry. The subject of this chapter, *integration,* is the practical way of accomplishing transparent communication with your audience in all levels of your ministry.

Your audience sees your social media channels as the ONE channel for all your ministry communication. For example, if you are a church, your audience would like to see what is happening with your worship team, your missions team and your management team. If you do not integrate social media with all departments, your social media team will not have the news from certain departments to share with your audience. And if you choose to project just one side of your ministry in those channels, then you are not making use of the opportunity to get your audience involved in multiple areas of your ministry. That is why integration is important. When you have content or updates about various aspects of your ministry, the audience is informed about all the facets of your ministry and able to connect with you at a deeper level.

The following sections examine specific ministry elements and how you can integrate them into social media.

SOCIAL MEDIA FOR SPECIAL EVENTS

Events are a great opportunity to integrate social media into all activities. You can start your social media activities right from the planning stage, for example you can conduct a poll on a couple of channels asking people which is the best venue in their city. You will be surprised by how much people love to contribute to ministries that involve them in decision making. During the preparatory stage, your social media team can post pictures and details of the preparations and the backstage activities, getting your audience excited about the event and involved long before the event even happens. Your audience will feel like they are walking with you step by step through this event, and the information they receive helps them advertise and promote the event among their circle, getting their friends and family involved.

Integrating your online and offline efforts surrounding a special event, from preparing online promotions to selling entry tickets to getting feedback online, can help you create that perfect event. Start by creating a dedicated webpage for each event, and if possible, distribute entry tickets or passes for the event using that home page. Also create an events page and provide specific information to the people who join the event. You can give them event-specific information, run promotions, and generally raise their expectations to make the event a big success.

During the event, record it and stream it live. Post live updates on various channels so that people who are not part of the event can participate and benefit from it. You amplify the impact of the event by taking it online, and you never know who you will reach. For example, the people in restricted countries or remote locations where there are no churches can participate in such events and be blessed.

After the event, a strong online presence can help you follow up with the attendees, stay in touch with them and continue to share useful information with them. These people may turn up for the next event, so it is a great idea to let them know that you are still in touch and you will keep them posted about the upcoming events.

SOCIAL MEDIA FOR REGULAR EVENTS AND CHURCH SERVICES

During regular ministry events or church services, remember that you have an online audience apart from the audience sitting in front of you inside the church building. Even within the online audience there are two types: one is the live audience who may be watching the social livestream or webcast, and the other is the on-demand audience who will consume the same content on their own time. For example, platforms like Facebook keep the livestream posted for people to watch and comment on whenever they like. And every week you can start promoting your church service by sharing the topic or even the gist of the message a week before, priming the audience and preparing them mentally before they get to the church. These promotions on social media will also help your audience invite other people who they think need to hear the sermon. For example, if you are going to share debt cancellation principles from the Bible based on the year of jubilee, you can prepare your audience by asking them on social media to think about their financial challenges and have their prayer points ready before they come on Sunday. They can inform their friends who may be in serious debt crisis and bring them along when they come to church. During the service, you could do some small things to get your social media audience involved, such as welcoming the Facebook or Periscope live audience along with your in-person church members. This is a good sign of integration.

Similarly, in addition to making ministry announcements on stage during your regular service, make those announcements in social media channels and on your website. Doing this regularly trains your audience to check for updates.

SOCIAL MEDIA FOR WORSHIP AND MUSIC MINISTRY

Music is very popular on social media and one of the most shared forms of content. If your worship team understands this and customises the songs and the worship session with the social media audience in mind, your ministry will benefit. Here are a few recommended actions to take surrounding music and worship services:

- Post the lyrics on social media to help people follow along. (Ensure you have the proper rights to do this. If you are a church, you can obtain a license from an organisation like CCLI[1])
- Involve the social media audience in selecting the songs for each service by conducting a poll or

having a social media post every Friday or Saturday inviting people to send their favorite praise and worship song list.

- Request feedback on each song from your social media audience.

- Post songs and lyrics before the service in order to teach your new songs to your congregation before they even get to church.

- Upload the songs after the service so your audience can share them with their friends and people connected to them. Record the songs and convert them into a social media-friendly format, and encourage people to leave comments and feedback.

SOCIAL MEDIA FOR PRAYER MINISTRY

Social media can be effectively used for your prayer ministry. When people are in need, social media can be a great tool to support and encourage them. Here are a few ideas of how to integrate your social media activity with prayer ministry:

- Create separate prayer channels on social media, such as a closed Facebook group for special prayers. The privacy will help people share confidential prayer points and pray for each other.

- If people give permission, you can share prayer points once a week on your public page and get the entire group of followers involved in praying for each other.

- Share testimonies on social media when you hear praise reports from people. This will encourage many people on social media in their walk with God and demonstrate the fruit of your ministry and how God is interested and involved in the lives of people.

- Provide tools like Whatsapp Groups or Facebook Messenger groups for your intercessory team to connect with each other regularly.

SOCIAL MEDIA FOR SMALL GROUPS MINISTRY

If you have cell group meetings and small group meetings for specific purposes, social media can be a good tool to keep the groups connected and functioning effectively. From scheduling time for the meeting to preparing topics to following up after meetings, you can do these tasks with social media. People can also stay connected to the group leaders and communicate with each other more easily. Social media can also be an efficient tool for the church management to monitor and manage the activities of multiple small groups, getting updates on the progress and empowering and nurturing those groups. For example, almost all social media channels offer a group facility, like Facebook Groups. As a ministry you can create an official Facebook group for each small group and assign church staff to moderate it. This arrangement gives you better access to each group and awareness of their needs and spiritual growth.

SOCIAL MEDIA FOR CHILDREN'S MINISTRY

Social media is one of the most suitable tools for children's ministry. Even though children must be of a certain age to directly participate on social media channels, you can still uses these tools to communicate with their parents or guardians and help children grow. You can share lessons and follow-ups with the parents not only on Sundays but throughout the week, encouraging them and helping them bring up their children with Godly principles. Share teaching resources and ask the parents to spend time with the children as they go through these resources. You can help parents network with each other using ministry-moderated social media channels and groups. You can use many types of visual medium like videos, design and infographics on social media to teach children.

These are some of the popular activities in ministries, but your ministry is unique and may have activities that you can adapt to social media in unique ways. Keep a list of those activities and brainstorm with your social media team ways of integrating social media into those activities.

———⌒———

To access additional resources, tools and information related to this chapter, visit
www.theconnectedchurch.org/tccbook/chapter8

CHAPTER 9

THE S.P.I.R.I.T. FRAMEWORK™ - RELEASING

Releasing is the act of giving wings to the content that you have carefully packaged, created and curated for your audience. It is the act of sending the content out into the great wide world of social media – but only after careful and meticulous planning.

The Bible says, 'I will send forth my word and it will never return to me void without accomplishing what I have sent it to do[1]'. You need to look at your content in the same way. When you create a good content, envision and dream about it going through the right medium, in the right format, and reaching the right audience, so that it will not come back to you without accomplishing what you have sent it to do. With the right planning, you can make this dream a reality.

CREATING A CAMPAIGN PLAN

One of the most organised and effective ways of releasing content into social media is by grouping it into campaigns. This is an approach that is widely used in the business, marketing and advertising worlds. As a ministry you can also adapt this approach for your social media efforts.

What is a campaign? A *campaign* is a focussed set of activities, usually with specific start and end dates, that has a single objective. It has a predefined set of promotional activities on various channels, using various content types, and is intended to accomplish a specific objective. You can have multiple campaigns running simultaneously or one after the other based on your plan and need.

For example, in your ministry, you could plan to have four different campaigns each week in the month of June. Each campaign can be aligned with the weekly sermon that you have prepared. You can even use the sermon title as the title of the campaign to strengthen that connection. All social media activities in that campaign should revolve around that topic. Let us assume that one week you speak about how to get out of debt. Your campaign plan could include a blog about the topic, multiple social media posts, a couple of short videos, a slide deck explaining the content, a podcast, a webinar, Snapchat and Instagram stories, and more on the same topic. All these activities form a single campaign even though there are multiple types of content and multiple ways in which the core concept of the original content is expressed.

The good thing about a campaign-based approach to releasing content is that it gives clarity to your team on what they should be focussing on at any given point in time. It also helps them plan for upcoming campaigns simply because they are able to see the entire schedule in their campaign plan. It helps streamline your content release activity on social media.

Tip: Give each campaign a unique code by which to identify it, and attach that code to all the content files in the campaign. This small step will help you track each campaign using tracking tools (which we will discuss in Chapter 11) and measure how it performed.

To quickly build up a campaign list open the structured goal sheet (we discussed in Chapter 6). Add channels to the sheet in one of the columns, assign responsibilities to the team and fix a release date for them. This will give you the set of campaigns that you can work on.

CREATING A SOCIAL MEDIA CALENDAR

Your campaign will have multiple activities, and each of them need a date and time. A social media calendar is where you slot the activities for specific dates and times. It is your map, providing an overall view of what needs to be accomplished during a specific period. If you think it would be beneficial to your team, you could drill down deeper and go into the exact tasks associated with each release of content. For example, in addition to placing the social media posting tasks in a calendar, you could include the preparatory tasks. If you have scheduled a blog post for 15th of June, then you need to have the blog content ready two to three weeks in advance in order to allow time to think about various ways of packaging it, designing suitable visual images to go with the content and preparing suitable posting content, hashtags, and so on. So list all of these tasks, give them dates and assign an owner. Now you have a set of preparatory tasks that need to be accomplished before the posting tasks come up. This level of detail will make your calendar a very practical and efficient tool. As a map, it will give you an idea of your workload and help you plan your resource allocation.

I suggest you design your entire workflow around your calendar. You can have a well-structured task list for your social media campaigns, but if those tasks are not assigned time slots, they are not going to get done.

Here is one approach to building your social media calendar, using the example of a church:

1. Schedule the guaranteed regular events for the entire year. You know there will be church service every week and a prayer meeting, for example.
2. Schedule special services for the year, such as Christmas, New Year's, Easter, Good Friday, and so on.
3. Schedule other planned ministry events like a harvest festival, fundraising event, missions

Sunday, children's program, leadership seminar, and so on.

4. Call for a meeting with all teams and departments in your ministry and request their department agendas for the year. Include those events and dates in the calendar.

5. Make some provisions for the events that may come up in the last minute. For example, you may get an invitation at the last minute to speak in a conference. Even though you may be a well-planned ministry, keep some buffer for surprises like these.

6. Consult your campaigns list and check to see that they are all covered in your calendar (most of them might be based on one or more of the above events, so they should be covered already). Add them to the calendar if needed.

7. Fill the calendar with the preparatory items for each event. Sit with your social media team and discuss how long it might take to prepare the content, visual elements and so on for each of these events, and work backward to fill up the calendar. For example, if it takes two or three days for you to create one blog post, then you should schedule it five to six days before the posting date. After you write the post, you may need to have someone proofread it, work on a promotional image to accompany it and send it to your team to post it after packaging it for marketing elements like hyperlinks, hashtags and more.

CREATING A PRE-RELEASE CHECK LIST

Before you release any content on social media, you need to ensure that it has some key elements with specific functionality:

- **A link back to your hub:** Almost all content that you send out on social media needs to have a link back to your content hub – either the website or a blog. Why? Because what the audience will see on social media is only a sample of the entire content. For example, a short quote will be posted from your 30-minute sermon on 'How to get out of debt'. Suppose your audience sees the quote and wants to know more. How will they access it? If you add a link back to your website, then your audience can click on it and learn more.

- **Tracking codes:** There are special tools to help you measure how many people come to your content hub (website or blog) using a specific link. An example of such a tool is the UTM builder.

- **Hashtags:** You are probably somewhat familiar with hashtags, which are words preceded by this symbol, #, and used on social media. Hashtags are a unique and effective way of gathering content related to a particular topic, so you should create or include existing ones that are relevant to your content.

TOOLS FOR RELEASING AND SCHEDULING

Finally, one of the key success factors in your release strategy is the set of tools that you use to release your content on social media. Even if you are an individual or a small ministry, unless you decide to use only one channel, posting content individually on each social media channel is time consuming. There are a number of websites that allow you to upload content and post to a variety of platforms simultaneously to simplify your workflow. The market is full of free and paid social media management tools catering to your needs based on your budget and requirements.

———————～———————

To access additional resources, tools and information related to this chapter, visit
www.theconnectedchurch.org/tccbook/chapter9

CHAPTER 10

THE S.P.I.R.I.T. FRAMEWORK™ - IGNITING

Can you imagine a Sunday when you prepare well and get ready to preach one of the most powerful, impactful and useful sermons you have ever preached, and you find that the church building is empty?

It happens all the time on social media.

There are times when ministers and church leaders spend hours and days preparing good content that no one sees. Why? Because their content gets drowned in the big ocean of social media, buried under a million other blog posts, podcasts and videos. Social media is getting noisier by the day.

The rate of increase in content volume is so high that the world's top social media influencers and visionaries are a bit concerned about the limited ability of people to consume content and the high rate at which content is produced.

So, by themselves, all the steps discussed so far in this book, including structuring, packaging, integrating and releasing, will not be enough to produce the best results for your ministry on social media. There is simply too much content out there.

What is the solution? Content ignition.

You need to *ignite* your content. I like the word 'ignite' because it is the act of setting something on fire – and anything on fire is hard to ignore! I believe that Christian life should be an ignited life. I believe that is why the Holy Spirit appeared in the form of 'tongues of fire' on the day of Pentecost.

But how do you set your ministry content on fire on social media? You need an ignition trigger – something like a lighter or matchstick that sets it ablaze. Even on the day of Pentecost, Peter had to preach the sermon that acted as the 'trigger' that made the fire of tongues come down. Here are 10 possible content ignition triggers for your ministry content:

TRIGGER #1 – USING THE UNIQUENESS OF YOUR CALLING

God created us in a unique way, and he has called each of us to unique ministries. Even though we all have the same Bible as the source of our ministry, no two of us minister in the same style. Your unique style can be an ignition trigger for social media. The social media world is always friendly and open to individuals who are genuine, authentic, real and unique. So I suggest you stop trying to imitate another star preacher or be someone else. Just be yourself. Create content that is unique to you. Deliver the content in a way that is unique to you. Think about how you can put the seal and mark of who you are and what God has placed inside of you in your social media content. This uniqueness will act as a trigger for your content and help you stand out in the crowd.

TRIGGER #2 – TAKING HELP FROM YOUR FIRST-CIRCLE AUDIENCE

Everyone has a primary group of audience in their ministry. It could simply be the friends and family who stood with you when you started. I remember when I started my workplace ministry and would conduct a weekly Bible teaching session for working professionals and business owners. Some days I had only one person in the room – and that was my wife! On some other days, it was just me and the chairs.

If you have been in ministry for some time, you probably have a regular audience already connected with your ministry. Even if you are starting fresh, you have your friends and family. This first audience can be your ignition trigger if you get them engaged in your posts.

The social media engine is designed to get cranking only when, at minimum, three criteria are met: The audience on your network must start *interacting*, *engaging* and *sharing* your content. You can accomplish these three requirements with your first set of audience. For example, if you are a church, you have your members who are already your audience; they already know you, like you, trust you and are ready to talk about you and share your content with others. Whenever you post your content, make sure that it reaches this group of people first. As your loyal audience, they will like, comment, share and start the ignition process for your content, widening its reach.

TRIGGER #3 – OPTIMISING YOUR CONTENT-HUB

Your content will be hosted in one place that will act as a hub. In most cases this is your website or your blog site. Optimise this content-hub so that it can act as your ignition trigger. You can optimise it in a number of different ways:

- **Adding a share button on pages.** A share button makes it easy for your audience to share the content that they see. 'Sharing' is the ultimate expression of love on social media, when someone shares your content they loudly say that they trust you and are willing to personally vouch for you. So make it easy for them.

- **Providing sharing options within the content.** Within your content (say, a blog post) you can give options for your audience to share just a specific part of your content. For example, when you have tweetable quotes in your blog post, you can add a feature that enables the reader to tweet it out using their Twitter account with just a couple of clicks. Software like Click to Tweet can help you implement such a feature on your website.

- **Adding sharing options to images.** You can use software or plugins to add sharing options that will appear when the audience clicks on or hovers over visual elements on your content. For example, you can place 'Pin It' buttons on your blog images so that users from Pinterest can share your images on their Pinterest boards easily.

- **Adding a 'similar content' or 'related content' section.** Visitors can see links to similar content at the end of your blog posts or pieces of content. These easy-to-follow suggested links help people to continue reading and eventually share and ignite the content. For example, if people are reading your blog on parenting, you can add other blog posts on family at the end of the page. This will help them read more content and eventually share it on their networks, initiating the trigger.

Ask your technology team to implement these simple features when you develop your website or blog site so that you can use your content-hub as your ignition trigger.

TRIGGER #4 – AMPLIFYING SHORTER VERSIONS OF YOUR CONTENT

Your ministry content may be packed with lot of information, but pulling out key highlights from all of your content to promote on social media can serve as an ignition trigger and help you reach more people. For example, take a 30-minute sermon and look for the 2- to 3-minute clips in which you focus on a key point, edit them out of your full-length video and promote those short clips on various channels.

TRIGGER #5 – PROMOTING REAL-LIFE STORIES AND TESTIMONIES

As a ministry, you should consider sharing testimonies on social media any time you hear them. There is nothing more powerful and helpful to others than hearing the story of another person who has gone through similar problems and overcome them. Real-life stories and testimonies can be good triggers, and they will help you increase your reach.

TRIGGER #6 – HAVING INTERACTIVE ELEMENTS

People love being heard. Include interactive elements as part of your social media content. Interactive elements can include polls, contests and quizzes. When people participate in these campaigns, their networks get notified, thus increasing the reach of your social media activity. When people get involved, they want their network to know that they are involved and they may even want to compare results, so they will share your interactive elements with others.

TRIGGER #7 – PROMOTING YOUR EVERGREEN CONTENT

If you have sermons and ministry materials that have created a big impact in the past, do not hesitate to reuse them. They can be a good ignition trigger on social media. If it worked for you before, it will surely work for you again in the social media era, as long as the message is still relevant. Over time, the areas of life in which people face challenges remain the same, and the source of the answers – God and the Bible – remains the same. Only the medium changes. So most of your Bible-based content is evergreen content. Do not hesitate to use your popular ministry content repeatedly in your social media campaigns.

———————⌒————

To access additional resources, tools and information related to this chapter, visit
www.theconnectedchurch.org/tccbook/chapter10

CHAPTER 11

THE S.P.I.R.I.T. FRAMEWORK™ - TRACKING

Now that you are fully equipped for social media ministry, you will soon be blogging, posting and tweeting on various channels. How will you know what works and what does not? This is where the last step of the S.P.I.R.I.T. Framework™ comes in.

WHY TRACK AND MEASURE?

Here is a list of reasons why you should track and measure your social media efforts on a regular basis:

- **Measurement helps you wake up before it's too late.** Social media efforts consume a lot of time, effort and resources. If you do not track key metrics and their performance regularly, you may be going off-track investing a lot of time and resources without realising it for months.

- **Measurement helps you step out and review progress.** Social media can be so interesting and engrossing that you and your team may be focussed on creating good content and engaging with your audience for long periods of time without reviewing your progress. Having a tracking and measurement schedule can help you step out of your routine and review your progress.
- **Measurement helps you plan.** Tracking and measuring the impact of your social media efforts and results not only helps you fine tune your current activities but also helps you plan your resources for the future.
- **Measurement is part of good stewardship.** God wants us to be good stewards of our time, effort and resources. These are gifts that came from him. Only if we track, measure and direct our resources at the right direction can we ensure that we are being good stewards of all that He entrusted us with.

PREPARING YOUR MINISTRY FOR SOCIAL MEDIA MEASUREMENT

Here are 7 steps that can help you prepare your ministry for tracking and measurement:

1. **Set aside time.** Devote a few minutes or even hours on a regular basis to tracking your progress. You have to purposefully create a schedule to track your social media progress on a

regular basis – once or twice a week or whatever frequency suits your ministry, as long as it's regular. If you are an organisation, schedule regular weekly and monthly review meetings in which your team presents the efforts taken and the results achieved.

2. **Start learning.** There are many measurement tools and many ways to measure social media efforts; you will not know which tools work for you or which method works for you until you learn about them and try them out. You must be willing to take time to learn about the tools that you choose, organise training programs (online and offline) for your social media team or maybe give them access to online courses and conferences. At the end of this chapter, we will discuss some of the learning tools and resources available.

3. **Decide to invest.** The right metrics at the right time can give you revelations that could change your ministry forever and increase your reach and impact. So, be ready to invest not just time but money, resources and effort into this task of measurement. You may have to purchase tools or subscribe to measurement services, or you may even need to hire a consultant in order to get the best data and feedback on your social media efforts. Your investment in these areas is money well spent.

4. **Choose the right tools.** Measurement tools are important. With multiple channels and hundreds of posts, tracking social media effectiveness can

be challenging. Even though this area is still evolving, there are some good tools available in the market that will give you useful dashboards and insights. Invest in them and use them regularly.

5. **List measurable objectives.** This is good time to go back to Chapter 6 and look at the core purpose, community, goals and KPIs from that goal sheet, and pick out the outcome or objectives that you would like to measure. For example, you may want to pay particular attention to certain goals and KPIs like church membership growth, growth of online followers, increase in engagement level, increase in reach, growth in donations, website visitor growth, email signups, or Bible college enrollment growth. Review this list regularly.

6. **Get offline feedback.** Set up a good offline feedback mechanism for your ministry. Allow your audience to freely express their thoughts and opinions anytime. Make provisions inside your church or in your office for people to walk in and leave their feedback. You may want to print feedback forms and make them available. Some people prefer anonymous communications and may give you valuable feedback that they may hesitate to discuss in person. Sometimes this direct feedback is more valuable than expensive measurement software. You could also make announcements asking people to give you feedback, letting them know that you are open to inputs on how your ministry is progressing.

Sometime telling people that you are open to criticism or negative feedback can have a big impact. Those inputs can be valuable. Since social media measurement is still an evolving field, there are many gray areas and the measurement process may not give you the complete picture. Close interaction with your audience and getting their feedback is one of the best measurement strategies.

7. **Be patient.** Social media results take time. It's a long-term investment, so be patient in your measurement process. Don't be discouraged when you don't have big numbers even after lots of effort. If you are doing things right, the seeds will produce a harvest. But any good sower knows that there is a time gap between sowing and reaping. That is simply how it works. So be open and willing to take the time to sow the right seeds, labour and wait to reap a good harvest.

WHAT TO TRACK AND MEASURE ON SOCIAL MEDIA

Since social media has many moving parts, you need to have clarity on what to track and measure. Every social media channel has its own set of metrics and there is no end to the amount of time you can spend measuring them. But I recommend that in the beginning you just focus on a few key metrics that are most relevant to your organisation and ministry goals.

There are 3 key factors that give you insight into the audience behaviour in social media:

- How people find you using social media
- How they interact with you after they find you
- How (or whether) they perform the actions that you want them to perform after they interact with you

Let us look at how you can measure each of them. I am going to use a tool called Google Analytics to demonstrate this measurement process.

Why Google Analytics? There are many tools and resources available for social media measurement (see end of this chapter for a list). And you can use any tool to measure these 3 factors. But the reason I chose Google Analytics to demonstrate is because it integrates closely with your website, which is your content hub – the place where all your social media activities culminate. So understanding how a tool like Google Analytics works is a great place to start your tracking and measurement journey.

Signing up for Google Analytics:

1. Register for a free Google account (skip this if you have an existing account). Tip: I recommend that you use a ministry Google account instead of a personal Google account to make things easier when you need to share the account details with other team members.

2. Visit analytics.google.com and sign up for a free Google Analytics account. You will see many paid premium services, but start with the free version (you can always upgrade later).

3. Connect Google Analytics to your website. This is as simple as pasting a tracking code on the backend of the website on all pages, and your web developer should be able to do this for you. Or see our resources page (details at the end of this chapter) for a step-by-step tutorial on how to do this.

Now you are all set.

Tip: I suggest you wait a couple of weeks or even a month after setting up Google Analytics before you start checking the results so that you will have enough data to make meaningful inferences.

Measuring how your audience found you - The Source and the Medium

A few weeks after setup, when you open your Google Analytics dashboard and you start seeing some numbers in it, then you know that your potential customers are starting to visit and interact with your website.

Now you need to know how they found you. Which social media channels or search engines did they use as a source and medium to locate your ministry? Among the millions of sites that are out there, how did your audience land up on your website?

The data on the source of your traffic and the medium can tell you which social media activity is bringing you visitors and which is not. With this knowledge, you can make an informed, data-driven decision on your social media efforts. For example, if your Google Analytics report shows that more visitors are landing on your website from a particular social media channel, then you can make a data-driven decision to increase your efforts in that particular channel, create more content for that channel, place ads and/or invest in a new content marketing campaign.

In Google Analytics, you can measure various sources of website traffic by looking in two places:

- **The 'Audience' tab:** This tab gives you an overview of your audience's demographics, including age and gender. You can also see their location details like city and country along with type of device and browser that they used to find you.
- **The 'Acquisition' tab:** In this tab you get an overview of the channels through which your visitors came to your website, with a breakdown by channel and source/medium. You can also look at the social media channels and the campaigns that are driving traffic to your website.

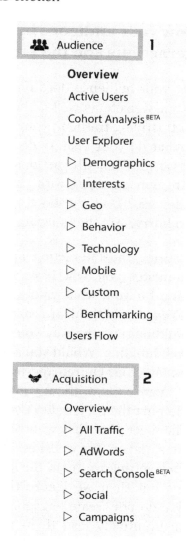

Measuring how your audience interact with you - The Interactions and the Engagement

Measure what your audience does on your channels after they find your website as well as how they engage with your content. Driving traffic to your website is only the beginning. What do your visitors do after they land on the website? Do they take the actions that you want them to take? Are they engaging with your content? Do they like what they see? Do they stay for a long time or do they leave in a hurry? Are they sharing your content?

Without measuring the interaction and engagement metrics, as a ministry you will have no idea which content is working for you, what your visitors like and what they don't. You should think of your website as your online church building, just the way you would think of your offline church building. Would you allow the church members to walk into your church and just hang around in the middle by themselves, without you or your staff or any volunteers helping them? Wouldn't you talk to them and try to help them get what they want? Yet, many of us make this very mistake on our websites. We spend a lot of time and money getting traffic to the site using social media campaigns but then we ignore the visitor after they get there. We do not create engaging, user-friendly content that will eventually lead them to the product, service or information that they seek. When you measure key interaction and engagement metrics, this data will help you understand your audience's behavior and help you serve them meaningfully.

In Google Analytics, you can look for various behavioral metrics in three places:

- **The 'Real Time' tab:** This tab is helpful if you have a time-specific event or activity. This tab shows you the 'active users' in real time, with their locations, the pages that they are visiting, the devices that they are using, and more.

- **The 'Audience' tab:** Under this tab, you can see the numbers for new vs. returning users, the frequency, the recency and the engagement in terms of session duration (the time spent by your audience) and page depth (the number of pages they visited).

- **The 'Behavior' Tab:** This tab has some of my favorite metrics and cool tools like 'Behavior Flow', a flowchart that shows you how your audience started and how they moved through your site with 1st, 2nd and 3rd interactions. This data can give you great insights into the behavior of your online audience. This tab also reveals which pages your audience visited, which page they were on when they left the site and much more. Make full use of this tab.

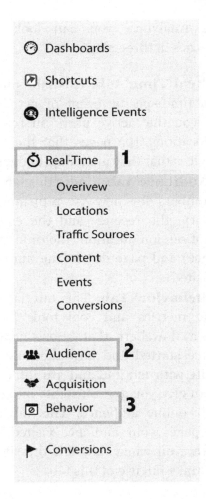

Measuring how your audience transact with you - The Conversion and the Cost

Finally, measure the most important metric for a ministry: conversion. This is obviously not *conversion* from a religious perspective but rather the measure of how all the efforts on social media and elsewhere online are converted into results by fulfilling our end goal objective.

For example, when you post a promotional image of a special event on Facebook, people clicking the 'LIKE' button on that post is an *engagement* activity. But after that, if they click the link inside the post and sign up for the event, then you have a *conversion*. When you measure this *conversion,* you should also measure what it *cost* you to get that conversion.

As a ministry, you should not lose sight of the end objective amidst all the activities and excitement of campaigns. The end objective for your ministry could be an event sign up, filling up a decision card, membership sign up, subscription, donation, email sign up, a product purchase or an eBook download – it could be a micro or a macro conversion. A micro conversion is a small step that leads to macro conversion, a big step. For example, someone watching your video where you talk about donations for your church building is a *micro* conversion. When they watch the video and decide to click on the donate button and donate, that is a *macro* conversion.

Google Analytics has a main 'Conversions' tab that helps you look at the 'Goals' that you have set and what it cost you to achieve these goals. You can set up either an assumptive or an actual pricing parameter for this section.

Social Media Measurement Tools and Resources

Apart from Google Analytics, there are many social media measurement tools in the market and there are new ones being launched each day. You can choose your tools depending on your preference, your operations, your team size and how you like to view the data of your social media ministry.

- **Direct tools from social media channels** – Almost every social media channel has their own measurement and analytics tool. Facebook Insights is one of the best tools on the market. It gives deep insights into all your posts, campaigns, etc. Twitter, LinkedIn, Pinterest and YouTube all have their own analytic tools.
- **Dashboard tools** – Since you may be working on more than one social media channels, you may like to look at all your social media data in one single place. There are tools like Google Analytics, Simply Measured and Kissmetrics that will collect all the data and present it to you in a Dashboard format.
- **Latest updates, news and useful resources** - Since social media is an ever-changing field, my team and I update *The Connected Church* website on a regular basis to give you latest updates and insights into specific social media and technology related topics and news. Visit www.theconnectedchurch.org/news to get all the latest news and updates.

- **Forum and communities** - In addition to the resources we also have a forum where you can ask questions and get answers from other users and experts. We also have private groups and communities on various social media channels where you can interact with other brothers and sisters who are interested in seeing the Church grow using social media and technology. Visit www.theconnectedchurch.org/connect to find out more about the forums and communities.

———— ∾ ————

To access additional resources, tools, tutorials and information related to this chapter, visit
www.theconnectedchurch.org/tccbook/chapter11

SECTION 4

FUTURE TRENDS THAT WILL IMPACT THE CHURCH

CHAPTER 12

FUTURE TRENDS

I believe God likes his people to be prepared for the future. The Bible is full of instances where He gives his people insights into the future through visions and prophecies, helping them prepare for what is coming. Today, if we as a Church prayerfully consider and watch certain technological trends, with God's help we can understand what is coming.

Even though this book is about social media, in this chapter I zoom out a bit to discuss broader technology trends that might have an impact on the future of social media directly or indirectly. These trends raise a lot of questions, and I do not try to give you all the answers (I do not have them!). But I do hope that knowing about these key trends will help us think together as a Church and find ways of solving the problems prayerfully, with God's guidance.

BEHAVIOURAL TRENDS: CHALLENGES AND OPPORTUNITIES

Attention span

One study shows that humans have shorter attention spans than goldfish! The study says[1] that in the year 2000, human beings had 12 seconds of average attention span, and it decreased to 8 seconds by 2015 thanks to all the gadgets and technology available. (By the way, a goldfish's attention span is 9 seconds!)

A short attention span that's just getting shorter raises a few questions for your ministry:

- How will you preach the Gospel to a generation with just 8 seconds of attention span?
- How will you teach biblical principles that take time, patience and discipline to learn and practice?
- How can you help this distracted generation understand that the key to solving their life problems is to focus on the scriptures?
- How will you get their attention and retain that attention?

The strategies discussed in earlier chapters, like visual content, short-form content and the funnel, may be the answer to some of these questions. But I would like you to consider these questions carefully and think of ways that you can overcome these challenges in your ministry, so that we do not become irrelevant for the coming generation.

Quiet and wrong influence

The coming generation runs the risk of being 'quietly' influenced by the wrong sources without the church even realising it. It is already happening in families. Many parents are not aware of how their children are being influenced by the content on social media. As I mentioned in the preface of this book, this is a *headphone generation* that is becoming more and more engrossed by the content on their mobile phones; they look down at their devices more than they look up at real faces. And the internet is full of content that is intended to influence its audience in ways that could be constructive or destructive. This trend will continue and only become stronger over time. As a Church, if we do not open our eyes and do something about it, then we are at risk of losing the next generation's attention altogether. In the next chapter we will look at some of the preparatory steps you can take as a ministry.

Open-mindedness

There is a wave of open-mindedness and a culture of acceptance in the world today, and in many ways that is a good thing. People are asked to be open about the way they think about various aspects of society. This trend is both an opportunity and a challenge to the Church. The open-mindedness opens the doors for the Church to share what it believes in and what it stands for. But at the same time, open-mindedness opens doors for distractions that might be easier to follow than what the Bible offers, thus attracting more attention. Of course, this is not a new phenomenon, and the Church has indeed overcome these challenges in the past. But this is an important factor for the Church to consider and think about in the coming days.

The open-mindedness of the future also means that the coming generation will be exposed to various paradigms and perspectives that many of us were never exposed to. Young people will ask questions we never asked. As a Church, are we ready to answer those questions? If we are not, or if we do not represent the truth convincingly, we risk losing our credibility and the attention of the next generation. I am not saying we should only tell them what they like to hear. My question is: How can you represent the truth in a relevant manner without diluting any of the core values or the principles of God's word? Can you use delivery methods and presentation techniques that are appealing to the connected generation, while retaining the power and essence of the life-saving truths of the Gospel?

Need for constant value-addition

As social media and technology open up the doors for people to access resources from around the world, the future generation gets used to very high quality of content and delivery techniques from outside the Church. Consider the way we present ideas, the logical reasoning, the scientific approach, teaching methodology and visual learning techniques. As a Church, are we equipped and prepared to present the truth in a high-quality manner that appeals to the coming generation?

The trends also indicate that people want content creators and influencers to get straight to the point, and they look for value in all that they consume. The future audience will have less time for anyone who is beating around the bush simply because the number of hours in their day remains the same and there are too many voices vying for their attention. As a Church, are we ready to get straight to the point, communicate clearly and powerfully and deliver value to people who connect online or offline?

TECHNOLOGICAL TRENDS: CHALLENGES AND OPPORTUNITIES

Growth in connectivity

At the time of this writing, only 50.1% of the world's population has access to the internet[2] (as of June 2016), but a study conducted by the World Economic Forum[3] indicates that by 2025, there is a high probability of us seeing 90% of the world's population having regular access to the Internet and 90% of the population using a smartphone.

These projections reveal a great opportunity for ministries to reach out to more people online. The best part of online ministry is that there are no limits – you can minister to any number of people, from any part of the world, at any time of the day without having to be physically present where they are. If you have the right setup, a value-adding message and a good workflow, then you can reach millions of people around the world and minister to them at a minimal cost.

Even if the type of ministry you are in is designed only for people who are physically present in front of you, that audience will also be online and connected, so you can still use the power of connectivity to better minister to them and be more relevant. For example, in your live events, you can use social media to answer questions from the audience. There are many ways to engage with your live audience using social media and technology. This trend will only continue and grow in the days to come.

Internet of Things

Internet of Things, or IoT, is a term used to refer to devices that are networked and connected to each other using internet. For example, until fairly recently, watches were only mechanical or electronic standalone devices, but because they are now connected to the internet in the form of smart watches, their functionality has expanded. A smart watch can tell you the weather of any city accurately, can help you measure your heart rate using your pulse on the wrist and send a text message to your doctor, can silently vibrate and alert you when there is a text message for you on your phone and more. Similarly, there are many electronic home appliances that can be connected to the internet. You can switch on your home air conditioner using an app on your phone so that the house is at the right temperature when you enter. One company recently showcased its smart refrigerator that can scan the items inside your refrigerator and alert you when you have to buy more milk or other groceries. It can even order them for you so that the items will be waiting on your doorstep when you get home. But all these are only the beginning of the IoT revolution, and more and more devices are being connected to the internet. Soon all the devices in your home, church and office will be connected to each other and communicating.

You can seize the opportunity of IoT technology and use it in multiple ways for ministry. High-resolution cameras that are internet-enabled can be fixed in certain locations to capture your church service and special events automatically. You can then simply stream them live on the internet directly using a wireless connection. You may not even need a computer and a person to manage all the broadcasting equipment. You can also use IoT in your church infrastructure for things like parking, seating, air conditioning and audio visual equipment to better control these elements and use them to deliver the truth in the most effective way to people.

Electronic money

You might have already heard of the words like *Bitcoin*[4], which is a 'cryptocurrency' that works on a technology called 'Blockchain'. It is expected that this technology will heavily influence the financial industry in the future. It is a currency that is created and held electronically, not printed like euros or dollars. It can be used to buy things electronically. The important thing that makes it different to conventional money is that no single institution controls the currency network.

Without getting too deep into technical aspects, it is safe to predict that the way people handle money will radically change in the future. This change will impact church donations, funding and the way people support ministries financially.

Financial sowing and reaping will continue to be a big part of Kingdom-building, but it will be carried out differently. As a ministry, you need to be alert, aware and ready to learn and embrace new financial services and tools so that people can participate in the church growth financially without difficulty. For example, when most people use a credit or debit card to handle money in their daily life and you do not have the ability to accept donations by credit card, you are hindering donors' ability to participate in your ministry financially. That is why it is important to be alert and aware of all future trends concerning money and finances.

Security, hacking and cyber protection

Among churches, when I talk about technology I always perceive sense a 'fear'. For some reason, as a Church we have learned to focus on the bad side of technology, and we think that the devil will try to use it to destroy the Church in these end times. This is partly true, and it is highly possible that the devil will try to use technology more in these end times. But here are some questions for you to think about:

- What if the Church uses technology more than the devil? In fact, I think the devil is freely using it because the Church is not!
- What if we who have the light occupy more space online than the sources that are influenced by the darkness? Where light is, darkness cannot prevail, right? So the more the church uses technology I think the less room there is for the powers of darkness to wrongly influence people and lead them to destruction.

While we talk about all the areas of excitement in the future, we should also look at some of the areas of caution. While we are in the process of occupying more space, we should also learn to protect ourselves from the existing problems of technology. For example, as connectivity increases within your ministry, your website, mobile apps, operations, databases and finances will be interconnected. A cyberattack and hacking of one system can create bigger impact in multiple systems. So as a ministry, when you plan your online presence, spend time thinking about how secure your setup is, hire consultants and experts to plug any open spaces in technology, take measures to back up your data regularly and take steps to not leave any doors open for hacking or cyber threats.

Language and translation technology

Words and languages are the foundation of all that we do in ministry. That is why I am fascinated with the developments in language and translation technology.

One company launched a crowd-funding campaign for its product, which is an earpiece that instantly translates what you hear in one language into another language of your choice. For example, you deliver your church sermon in English. One of your church audience members who knows only French can plug this into his ear, switch on the app and hear your entire sermon in French, as you speak. The earpiece will translate the sermon in real time! These types of translation technologies are still under development, but when they are out in the market, the language barrier for ministry that exists today will vanish. You will be able to minister to people from any part of the world without worrying about which language they speak. What an opportunity for Kingdom-building!

Innovations in transportation: Self-driving cars, jetpacks and hovering devices

The transportation industry is going through a revolution. Self-driving cars are already being tested on the roads. One company is even testing 'jet engine-powered' backpacks that allow the wearer to fly. Another company is testing a Star Trek-type of 'hovering' vehicle that can move you from place to place without touching the ground. Even though these technologies are in the early stages of development, they indicate how transportation and logistics will change in the future. Covering physical distances will not be a concern. From a ministry point of view, the way people come for your events, seminars and conferences will change. If you have the right message, people will be able to find you and attend your ministry meetings irrespective of the distance.

If you are a missionary, with these advancements you will be able to travel to any place in the world and help any group of people no matter the distance. You will be able to take the good news quickly to any corner of the globe, removing many limitations of ministry faced in the past.

Virtual reality, augmented reality and hybrid reality

You might have heard of the phenomenal success of the app Pokemon[5], which superimposes virtual characters into your real life environment via your smartphone. Open the app and point your smartphone camera to your street, and you'll see a little animated character on your street that you can catch using the app. This gets very interesting when other people who use the app also see the character in the same place as you do. Then you both can interact with that character at the same time.

Superimposing one reality on another is called *augmented reality*. Similarly there are other reality technologies, like *virtual reality,* or VR, which allow you to become a part of a particular scenario. For example, you can sit at home, wear a virtual reality headset and watch a football game while feeling like you are in the stadium watching the game live. These are immersive experiences. Since you are wearing a headset, there are no other distractions and you are fully immersed in that reality. And all of this technology is now becoming affordable and available in the market.

Let us imagine that you are preaching your sermon in your church to the audience sitting in front of you. If you have a 360-degree camera that can capture your church sermon and livestream it (using technology that is already available in the market), anyone around the world can simply wear their VR headset and be virtually inside your church while you are preaching! It is the closest thing to actually being present in church. With their VR headsets on, the VR audience can turn to the left or right and see other church members in real time. They can listen to the sermon and take notes sitting at home. You can minister to them from anywhere as long as they have internet and the VR headset. What an amazing possibility! Very soon VR headsets will become regular household items, and many TV and movie producers are creating content for VR. When that happens you can build your church virtually. This kind of technology breaks all barriers that the church has faced and opens up unlimited possibility for ministries to help and service people. And it's not far in the future – it is coming soon.

As a Church, are we ready and fully equipped to take full advantage of these new opportunities?

———————— ∽ ————————

To access additional resources, tools and information related to this chapter, visit
www.theconnectedchurch.org/tccbook/chapter12

CHAPTER 13

FUTURE-PROOFING YOUR MINISTRY

In the online world, the old makes way for the new much more rapidly than in other walks of life. Change is a constant in social media. There is a perpetual hunger for evolution, and many entrepreneurs capitalise on that hunger by creating new companies, new products, new technologies, new user experiences and new social media channels. Nothing can stop this continuous stream of change – it is here to stay.

What can you do in the face of such constant change? 'Future-proof' your ministry by being prepared for any new social media or technological change that might come your way in the future.

When change comes, your response will have two parts: external and internal. Externally, you will take the required physical action to implement new processes, gadgets and workflows, deploying teams that can handle the change. But the other important part is your internal response – the way you think, operate, work, create, serve and function to deal with that change. The internal response is much more difficult and much more important then the external response because without internal preparations, you will not be able to undertake external activities. That is why this chapter focuses on how you, as a ministry, can prepare your internal response and respond well in the time of need. Let us look at a few preparatory steps you should take right now.

STEP #1: CREATE A CULTURE OF RELEVANCE

In social media, people spend significant amounts of their precious time reading email newsletters and blogs and watching videos of influencers. They devote this time and consume this content because it is relevant to their personal or work life. The day these influencers lose their relevance, they will lose their followers, too. Create a work culture in which you and your ministry team are constantly striving to be relevant to your audience. This effort will help you open up your mind to new ways of using social media, adopting latest technological advancements and embracing change to meet the needs of your audience.

A true heart of service is one that puts the needs of the person you are serving ahead of your needs. And you can serve another person with such a heart only if they allow you to be connected with them in some way. They will stay connected to you only if you stay relevant to them. Create a work culture in your organisation in which every employee or volunteer in your ministry understands the importance of being relevant, and train them on how they can be relevant to the people you serve. This effort will help you future-proof your ministry.

STEP #2: CREATE A CULTURE OF READINESS TO CHANGE

Always be ready to embrace the 'new'. Reducing the change resistance inside your ministry is an essential survival technique in this social media age. Ministries, individuals and businesses that resist change will face extinction in the online world. Nimble and flexible organisations will thrive and flourish. I know that change is not easy; it usually requires a big effort, and it can be a bit annoying, sometimes even painful. For example, if there is a new social media channel that most of your church members are using, then your ministry *has* to get on that channel. You may be required to change your video setup, the team that works on such things and many areas of your operations. You may even need to change the way you prepare and present your messages on the pulpit just for the sake of one more channel. While all of these changes can be painful, they are necessary if you truly want to serve people online. Anyone who refuses to change cannot truly serve.

Change is not a new concept for Christians. Christian living is all about change. We started our new life in Christ only when we first changed the way we thought about God, purpose, life, the cross and forgiveness of sins. 'Repentance' is our first step in Christianity; look closely at the root word 'repent' in the original language, and you will see that it means to 'think differently' or 'think upside down' or 'turn around', which essentially says we should change the way we think about life. Repentance is mostly associated with sin, but it can also be applied to all other areas of life. As children of God we need to start thinking differently about other areas of our life such as money, family, technology and work. The scriptures say that we as Christians are 'continually transformed by the renewal of our minds'. So ideally, building a culture of change in a Christian ministry from a social media and technology perspective should not be a big challenge. When you build such a culture of change in your ministry, then you don't have to worry about the future because you're prepared to handle any technological change or need that demands a new approach. If you lay this foundation as a leader, then your team will also be ready to embrace change without much resistance.

STEP #3: CREATE A CULTURE OF LISTENING

Social media and technology have allowed people to express themselves freely. Broadcasting your opinion and point of view to the entire world is as simple as clicking the 'live' button on a social media mobile app. While the ease of this technology is encouraging and empowering, sadly it has also given rise to people who are used to more talking and less listening. Communication is a two-way street, and it is only effective when you learn to listen. Most ministries are well-equipped to express their wisdom and talk about their specialisation to people on social media, but is that what you should be doing right away? Or should you be listening to your audience, learning what they want and then talking about the things that are relevant to them?

Listening should start long before you say the very first word on social media. Listening should be part of your initial preparation. Everything you do online should be based on what you have heard from your existing and potential audience. And even after you start broadcasting yourself on social media, you should continue to listen by requesting and accepting feedback (both good and bad), and keep changing your approach accordingly.

As a ministry leader, if you have a heart and ear that is ready to listen and if you build a team that operates in a culture of listening to others, then you will know what your audience needs. You will know when their preferences are changing, and you will know what they want from an online technology perspective (which social media they are using, which is their preferred medium of communication and so on). Then you can prepare to serve them in the relevant manner.

A quick note on handling critical comments: When you listen, you must be open to receiving criticism and negative feedback. As Christians, we are experts in the art of being nice. We think that the expression of love is all about saying nice things to people. Expression of love, as we can see from the life of Jesus, is not just about being nice, however, but about being right. You as a leader can practice saying the right things to people (with love) and learn to receive straight and honest feedback (which comes to you with love). This feedback will help you re-examine what you have implemented and consider how you can improve it. There will always be room for improvement in everything that you do as a ministry. If you do not have an open attitude to feedback and react sharply and defensively to every single criticism, then eventually people will stop telling you the right things, knowing it upsets you. You will lose the great opportunity of getting quality, honest feedback from your colleagues, users and ministry audience who love you. So keep yourself open and be ready to listen.

STEP #4: CREATE A CULTURE OF CURIOSITY

Be curious about social media, technology and new ways of doing things. Try things out and see what works for you and what does not. Almost all channels these days are constantly improving their technology and features. You have to be curious and ready to try out new things; keep abreast of the new features and work your social media plan around them. Build a team that is curious to learn the latest trends and techniques, too. When you try new things, you might make a few mistakes along the way, but that is better than never trying. I pray and hope that Christian ministries will soon become the early adopters of all kinds of technologies and innovation instead of playing catchup.

STEP #5: ATTRACT THE RIGHT TALENT

When God asked Moses to build the tabernacle in the middle of the wilderness and desert, he did not ask Moses to do it all by himself. He had the HR strategy and the recruitment plan in place. In the middle of the desert and among his own people, Moses found Bezalel and Aholiab ready with all the required skills[1]. Our God is an awesome provider of the right people at the right time. I have personally experienced it in my business and ministry time and again. As an organisation, you will also experience this grace. If God has called you to minister using social media, He will provide the right people and resources to get the job done.

But that is not to say that you don't also need to do your part and prepare your organisation by building a culture that will not only attract the right talent but also retain them. Work on your HR policies and create a workplace that encourages and nurtures people. Create an atmosphere that helps your staff grow and mature, both personally and in their careers. Many ministries focus on their congregation and audience so much that they have no time or energy to minister to their own staff. Equip your army properly or you are not going to win the battle. Take time to create a work environment that inspires creative ideas and does not stifle their creativity and potential. This is important especially for the members of your social media team, who need to come up with multiple ideas for multiple campaigns week after week, month after month.

While recruiting, always be fully aware of the specific needs of your social media and technology divisions. Keep your eyes open for the right kind of people. Let your current audience (like church members) know about openings so that they can refer people they know. Use the power of crowdsourcing to recruit the right talent. Keep looking for agencies, freelancers and consultants who can help you grow and expand.

Add recruitment as a regular prayer point in your ministry, and involve God in the process. Even when you don't have a specific opening, I recommend that you interview and meet people who approach your ministry looking for a job. You never know what talent you may find. Your senior management team could spend an hour or two each week having brief conversations with people who contact your ministry looking for jobs. You can be transparent to them about the fact that you do not have a specific role in mind but you would like to chat and explore options. Create a spreadsheet or an online record of all the interviews to build a repository of various talent. Then when you need someone specific, you can look through this database first. Building the right team is one of the most effective strategies for your ministry. You can handle any change if you have the right team with you.

STEP #6: CREATE A CULTURE OF LEARNING

Create an atmosphere that helps your ministry staff and volunteers grow on a regular basis. One of the best ways to do that, especially in your social media division, is to foster a culture of learning. Empower people to learn from each other and from external resources. Plan and help your staff go through training programs, online courses, certifications, conferences, seminars and webinars. Enabling them to learn new skills and update their knowledge will not only help them grow professionally, but it will also empower your ministry to stay up-to-date with current trends.

Promote interdepartmental learning within your ministry, where one department takes time to teach their overall approach and techniques to another department. They may not go into all the details, but they can give an overview of their work so that all departments are aware of each other's work and look for ways to contribute to their growth. During these interdepartmental learning sessions, ask the presenter to include the current challenges their department faces; they might get a fresh perspective on the solution from another department. Constant learning is good both for the present operational efficiency and for future-proofing of your ministry.

STEP #7: BE PART OF THE CONNECTED CHURCH NETWORK

As I discuss earlier in the book, there is power in staying connected with each other within the body of Christ. This is the most powerful future-proofing strategy for your ministry. Do not try to accomplish everything on your own; churches can work with other churches, missionaries can work with churches, workplace ministers and lay preachers can support missionaries, Christian nonprofits can get volunteers from churches or employ missionaries for part-time functions, you can partner with businesses that offer a specific service that you need — there are a million ways in which we as one body benefit when we are connected. We are more empowered to deal with our challenges as a community than by ourselves. And that is what our God wanted us to do: to live as one body, in Him. Christian symbols such as Holy Communion were given to us to emphasise the importance of living as a community.

Today, you can build a community both online and offline easily and effectively using technology and social media tools. Use existing tools like Facebook groups and Chat messengers, or custom-build a community of your own with membership websites and social network channels built into your own ministry website. But whatever the method you adopt, make sure that you stay connected with the community and work as a community — contributing, sharing, learning, giving, encouraging and empowering one another.

With these seven steps, your ministry will be well-equipped to handle all the challenges of new technology and social media evolution.

———————

To access additional resources, tools and information related to this chapter, visit
www.theconnectedchurch.org/tccbook/chapter13

CONCLUSION

A NEW SEASON

A s the body of Christ we are entering a new season. A season of change, a season of hope, a season of exciting new possibilities empowered by technology, connectivity and social media.

This season will help us serve the hurting, the poor and the needy in ways that was never possible before, by opening up doors of opportunity for us to collaborate seamlessly with our brothers and sisters from around the world. This season will increase our ability to go places and share the good news with people faster, more effectively and more efficiently than we were ever able to. Personally, for many of us this season will be a wave of change as we see new technologies and new social media channels come and occupy a big part of our everyday lives.

How will you respond to this season? Will you be overwhelmed and decide give up? Or will you raise up to the challenge, embrace the change and create an impact in this world? I strongly encourage you not to give up. The God who has been with you so far will continue to lead you and guide you through this too. After all, Jesus said 'I will be with you till the end of days'. The fact that you are holding this book in your hands (and that you have reached the last chapter) is proof that God is mightily at work in this world, raising up people who will learn and understand the functionalities of social media and all technological tools and will put them to good use for building His kingdom of love, peace and joy on this earth.

In these end times we may see some new destructive technologies, gadgets, ideas, teachings, distractions, attractions and innovations that will try to draw people away from the truth into destruction, but through you and me and by the Grace of God, the Word of God can prevail and continue to overpower all of them by shining the light of life into the hearts of human beings.

In technological hubs around the world, God is continuing to raise up 'Digital Moses'es who will lead people out of various types of slavery and bondage by proclaiming the truth of the Gospel online, creating valuable content and building businesses with Kingdom values (for-profit and nonprofit). Will you be one of those 'Digital Moses'es? Will you decide to work with God and help him deliver his people from the power of darkness into the Kingdom of light, using social media and technology?

Be strong, and be encouraged about the future. Focus on the calling that God has placed in your life, continuously work on improving your gifts and talents, and create content that will help others. Remember Paul's words, 'I have become all things to all people so that by all possible means I might save some'. Use all possible channels and techniques to spread and share the message of God's love with people who need to hear it — even if it is through VR headsets and wireless headphones.

Thank you for spending your precious time with me through this book. I sincerely hope it has added value to you. Now go implement all your learning and serve others using social media.

Stay connected. Stay blessed!

P.S. - Remember to make use of the many resources I have made available on the website www.theconnectedchurch.org to help you build a ministry that is technology & social media-savvy

www.theconnectedchurch.org

REFERENCES

CHAPTER 1

1. Source: http://www.marketplaceleaders.org/articles/jesus-was-a-workplace-minister/
2. Source: https://www.statista.com
3. Source: http://www.dailymail.co.uk/sciencetech/article-2449632/How-check-phone-The-average-person-does-110-times-DAY-6-seconds-evening.html

CHAPTER 2

1. Source: http://www.internetlivestats.com/google-search-statistics/
2. Source: The Book of Revelation 12:11
3. Source: The Gospel according to John 1:1

CHAPTER 3

1. See Matthew 28:18 to 20

CHAPTER 4

1. Genesis 2:23
2. Genesis 3:12
3. Source: Facebook Company Website http://newsroom.fb.com/company-info/

CHAPTER 6

1. Open Minds Agency – www.openmindsagency.com
2. Proverbs 1:5

CHAPTER 8

1. See: https://us.ccli.com/

CHAPTER 9

1. Isaiah 55:11

CHAPTER 12

1. Source: http://time.com/3858309/attention-spans-goldfish/
2. Source: http://www.internetworldstats.com/stats.htm
3. Source: http://www3.weforum.org/docs/WEF_GAC15_Deep_Shift_Software_Transform_Society.pdf
4. Source: https://en.wikipedia.org/wiki/Bitcoin
5. Source: https://en.wikipedia.org/wiki/Pok%C3%A9mon

CHAPTER 13

1. See Exodus 36

ACKNOWLEDGEMENTS

I first thank my Lord and Saviour Jesus Christ for everything; specially for his love, redeeming grace and presence in my life. As written in John 15:5, apart from him I can truly do nothing.

All that I know I have learnt from the people whom I have interacted with. So I am forever indebted to the many amazing men and women who have taught me, corrected me, helped me, inspired me and encouraged me: family, colleagues, bosses, mentors, clients, vendors, partners, teachers and friends.

To my dedicated and hardworking team in Open Minds Agency. I am so privileged to have in-house access to a highly talented creative, accounts, design, video, social media, marketing and technology team. I am thankful for you guys.

To my dear pastor Rev. Sam P. Chelladurai. Thank you for your life-transforming teaching and for the love, support and faith you have in me. I thank God for you!

To my dear friends, Rebecca and Mark Schaefer. Thank you for supporting and encouraging me through this journey. Your love for God's Kingdom, your humility and your heart to help others is so inspiring.

To my editor Elizabeth Rea. Thank you for being patient and making this book readable.

To my friend Samson and the team at Surrenden, Coonoor and the team in Cornerstone house, SU Family Ministries, Mahabalipuram, where I wrote most of this book. Thank you for your love, warmth and hospitality; you have a unique role in building God's Kingdom of love.

To the authors, speakers and creators of the many books, podcasts, online courses and conferences that I have learned from and continue to learn from. I specially thank Michael Stelzner, Social Media Examiner and Phil Mershon, Director of Social Media Marketing World, from where I have received much inspiration, knowledge, connections, encouragement and wisdom that helped me write this book.

To Lyn and Brett Johnson, my God-given family. Thank you for standing by me, supporting me, encouraging me, inspiring me, counselling me, praying for me and loving me unconditionally. I love you!

To Tina, the love of my life. Thank you for being my partner, my counsellor, my helper, my editor and my friend. Thank you for sharing the conception, pregnancy and labor pains with me as I gave birth to this book. You are a precious gift and I look forward to transforming the world with you!

ABOUT THE AUTHOR

Natchi Lazarus is a digital marketing consultant, social media strategist and a keynote speaker.

Natchi is an Engineering Graduate, has a Masters in Business Administration (M.B.A.) specialising in Marketing, and a Post-Graduate Diploma in International Business. He fell in love with marketing during his business school days, and worked with Ogilvy & Mather as a student trainee, where his love for marketing and advertising deepened. He held management positions in top corporate houses in India like ICICI Bank, TATA Group and BAJAJ Group before becoming a business consultant.

Now with more than 15 years of marketing experience, he spends most of his time and is passionate about helping businesses, nonprofits, churches, faith-based organisations and startups use the power of the internet and social media to amplify their message and reach their audience.

He has been researching and coaching working professionals and business owners on Biblical concepts of work for more than 10 years using his faith-based blog and teaching arm, <u>Word@Work</u>.

He is the cofounder of <u>Open Minds Agency</u>, a digital marketing agency working with businesses and nonprofits worldwide.

You can learn more about Natchi, his work, his spiritual journey & his online marketing adventures from his website <u>www.natchilazarus.com</u>. You can connect with him on Twitter <u>@natchilazarus.</u>